ADVERTISING
IN VICTORIAN ENGLAND
1837-1901

Diana and Geoffrey Hindley

Advertising

IN VICTORIAN ENGLAND 1837–1901

WAYLAND PUBLISHERS LONDON

To our parents

SBN 85340 047 4

This book first published in 1972 by
Wayland (Publishers) Ltd
101 Grays Inn Road London WC1

Printed in Great Britain by
C. Tinling & Co. Ltd, London and Prescot

CONTENTS

ILLUSTRATIONS

The Author and Publishers would like to thank the following for kindly loaning pictures for reproduction in this book. *Colour:* John Johnson Collection of the Bodleian Library, Oxford, plates C.1–C.7 and jacket picture; Rowntree Mackintosh Ltd, plate C.8. *Black and White:* Mansell Collection, plates 1.1a, 1.3a, 1.3c, 1.3d, 1.4b, 1.5, 1.6, 1.7, 1.8b, 1.10, 2.7, 2.12, 4.4, 5.8, 6.1, 6.5, 7.4b; Radio Times Hulton Picture Library, plates 1.1c, 1.3b, 1.9; London Transport Executive, plates 1.4a, 1.4c, 1.4d; Victoria & Albert Museum, plates 3.3, 3.4, 4.5, 8.1, 8.2, 8.4, 8.7; John Johnson Collection of the Bodleian Library, Oxford, plates 2.1–2.6, 2.11, 2.13, 3.8, 5.2, 5.9, 6.3, 6.9, 6.10, 7.1, Epilogue; Mary Evans Picture Library, plates 3.1, 6.7, 7.2b; Reckitt & Colman Ltd, plates 2.9, 2.14, 3.2, 7.7; Hovis Ltd, plate 3.1; Cadbury Schweppes Ltd, plates 3.5, 3.6; Bovril Ltd, plates 3.9, 3.10; Guinness Museum, plates 3.12, 3.13; Wills' Collection of Tobacco Antiquities, Bristol, England, plates 4.1, 4.2, 4.3; Beecham Group Ltd, plates 5.4, 5.6; Raymond Mander & Joe Mitchinson Theatre Collection, plate 8.3; A. & F. Pears Ltd, plate 7.10; John Freeman Ltd, plates 2.8, 3.7, 5.5.

I
THE MEDIA

As the nineteenth century advanced a group of men were struggling to win a place among the serried ranks of the respectable professions. Respectability was a highly prized attribute in Victorian England but these new men followed a calling which began with a reputation for sharper practice and which seemed, by its very nature, to require qualities of self assertion bordering on brashness. The new men were the advertising agents and their story occupies a big place in the chapters that follow.

Towards the end of our period the agents' quest for status was nearing its goal but, as a body of skilled and hard-working men, they had more practical and important problems on hand than mere prestige and vanity. For it was the advertising agents of the last century who worked out the basic services and responsibilities of the profession. One of the first services to be offered was expert knowledge of the media available. Because of this, and also because a survey of the media is one of the first requirements in any successful advertising campaign, we begin our book with a review of the media available to the advertiser.

In the days before the moving picture the scope of the advertiser was far more limited than it is today. Yet the Victorians had a fair number of possibilities open to them, and indeed one or two which are not available today. In the 1880s, for example, we find a tantalising reference in one agent's promotional literature to the use of lecturers as an advertising media – but how they were to be used is not clear. The Victorians made greater use of the poster than we do now – with our cinema and television screens – and even invented the sandwich man and advertising vehicle to carry posters through high streets where the absence of hoardings inhibited the activities of bill stickers. In the theatre the safety curtain was put to use as an advertising medium, a practice that was continued through into the 1950s. At least one agent, A. E. Abrahams of Forest Gate, London, advertised himself as the sole contractor of the Christmas pantomime curtains at all the best London suburban theatres.

Until the 1890s the range of media remained virtually unaltered. Then, innovations such as flashing electric signs and flicker moving pictures heralded the arrival of a new age and new techniques. Until then, however, the printed page in one form or another had been the preponderant advertising medium. For most of the eighteenth century taxes had been levied on newspapers and on their advertisements. Described by the newspaper proprietors, in somewhat sensational terms, as "taxes on knowledge" they did, along with the tax on paper, put a real brake on the development of the advertising industry. Some enterprising publishers like Edward Lloyd, anxious to capitalize on growing mass literacy and on the manufacturers' zeal for advertising, produced journals that carried fictitious reports of law trials and other imaginative material. These "journals" successfully evaded the tax on "newspapers". The newspaper tax thus worked against the public interest, not only by limiting the number of newspapers, but by actually putting a premium on misinformation.

The levy on advertisements was still more unreasonable. First, it was made only on announcements in newspapers. Journals and magazines – periodicals that did not have to be registered as newspapers – were exempt. Second, the tax was inequitable as between advertisers. Until 1833 the levy was charged at the rate of 3*s* 6*d* per item; in that year it was cut to 1*s* 6*d*. Since the tax was unrelated to the length of the advertisement or its subject, a half column announcement of the sale of a £100,000 country estate was taxed the same as a servant's two-line advertisement for a new position. Among many other absurdities was the fact that the tax could be levied on a favourable book review. In view of the exposure of "puffing" in *Ainsworth's Magazine*, described in Chapter Eight (The Arts of the Copywriter), the Treasury's reasons here are understandable; but so, too, would be the feelings of an author whose work was slated by an impecunious magazine.

The tax on newspapers, imposed by the Stamp Act of 1712, had risen as high as 2*d* per copy in 1815. But the political commotion of the Great Reform Bill of 1832 produced scores of fly-by-night unstamped "*Poor Man's Guardians*" and "*Democrats*" that made it plain that the enforcement of the law was not worth the revenue. In 1836 the stamp duty was reduced, and in 1855 scrapped. The immediate consequence was a sudden founding of new newspapers – made easier by growing national literacy. One, the *Daily Telegraph*, founded in 1855, battled through after initial difficulties. But there were many others which, after a brief struggle for circulations and advertisements, ignominiously sank from view.

The flood of new periodicals in the late 1850s increased the competition for advertisers. Some proprietors began over-stating their circulation figures to attract advertisements in their pages, while others adopted the opposite tactic of publishing the real figures certified by accountants. Others, more sophisticated yet, introduced the notion of "readership figures". Circulation figures could be quoted accurately, but were lent a new significance by the vast number of readers who were assumed to read each copy actually bought. Even today readership figures are not always considered indisputably reliable. In the nineteenth century they were often mere speculation. However, some specialist publications made claims that, while impressive and incontrovertible, were nevertheless vague. The publishers of *The Primitive Methodist*, for example, could honourably claim to be the official organ of a religious community of more than 200,000 adults, without specifying how many actually took the paper. Another interesting anticipation of the use of readership figures, today a regular practice, comes from the *Great Western Advertiser* of the 1840s; this was a controlled circulation advertiser that made a special point of the fact that it was distributed only to hotels and other public places where each copy was read by several readers. By 1900 the *Illustrated London News* was making still grander claims. "In every club in England you will see the *I.L.N.* In most big hotels you see it also and the result is that not only one individual who pays sixpence for it, but perhaps 50 or 60 people a day, turn over the pages and their eye is caught by some striking advertisement."

The *Illustrated London News* was launched in 1842 by Herbert Ingram, partly with the intention of cashing in on the popularity of picture magazines. Within two years it had achieved a circulation of 25,000. A new venture, the *Pictorial Times* of 1846, aimed to surpass even this, and announced a sensational promotion campaign – "Thousands of pounds sterling Given Away! !" The scheme worked like this: each annual subscriber to the *Pictorial Times* was given a receipt bearing a number; these numbers were drawn in a lottery and the winner was to receive £1,000. The same immense sum – worth perhaps ten times as much today – was to be paid to every ten thousandth subscriber. The scheme, which was carefully thought out, was a nice blend of the sensational and the practical. What success it had is not known.

Other less successful publishers had to use less dramatic methods. In the early 1860s a part work (serial publication) entitled *Beauties of the Coastland and Highland Scenery of Great Britain* proposed a way of recruiting advertisers which was as tortuous as its name. "Professional tradesmen," it announced, "are respectfully informed that by becoming advertisers in this work, they are entitled to an advertisement in each part gratuitously; by taking the book as published in monthly parts at two shillings each. All advertisements sent for insertion will be considered orders for the journal."

The finances of the *Family Friend* were a good deal healthier. After ten years of trading, this journal published an extract from its accounts, full of facts and figures, to impress its readers. Out of a total revenue of £95,500 sales produced £77,500 and advertising only £18,000, or about twenty per cent. As against this the paper spent no less than £10,000 in promoting and advertising itself.

In the 1860s, when advertisers and publishers were still discovering the potential of the new press, sharp practice flourished like the green bay tree. Since few of the pioneers understood what was possible and what was not, the fly operator found it easy enough to deceive even hard-headed businessmen who were used to getting the better of a bargain. One can imagine how zealously the confidence trickster exploited the public's fascination with the mysteries of advertising. One baited his trap with an enticing small ad which appeared for about three months in the personal columns of *The Times*: "Wanted, a young gentleman to act as traveller for advertisements among the best houses for a high class publication. The applicant shall be required to invest about £200 on first-class security. Apply 'Literary'." The interviews, short and to the point, were held in a fashionable office near London's Fleet Street – borrowed for the occasion – where each young enthusiast was offered an annual salary of £100 with a handsome commission, not to mention a ten per cent return on his "investment" in the publication. No fewer than six applicants were successful. When they all arrived on the appointed day to find a deserted office there were, we may assume, a number of "wry grimaces".

Young men with more money than sense were not the only ones willing to believe the impossible. In the heady years after the lifting of the newspaper and advertising taxes, scores of little publishers competed for advertisement revenue in an overexploited market. One appointed a canvassing agent: he gave him sole agency for the paper on a twenty-five per cent commission for multiple insertions of twenty-six or fifty-two weeks, but absolutely refused to pay any cash advances. Commission would be paid only if the agent could prove that advertisements had been contracted. Things went well for the first few weeks; the space salesman was able to establish his *bona fides* by taking orders from such well-known advertisers as Holloway's Pills. But then the supply dried up and, true to his word, the publisher refused to advance a penny until he had evidence of an order. The canvasser continues the story: "Now curiously enough, I had a few days before, at a pub used by canvassers, met a well-dressed man who informed me that he had started a patent medicine and was open to advertise it at any extent, provided he could get credit. His lack of cash did not concern me as far as commission was concerned. I agreed to fall in with his views and accept as many orders as he could favour me with. To cut a long story short I presented my friend the religious publisher with a contract note, of which the following may be taken as a copy: 'Please insert our advertisement in your paper to occupy one column for 52 weeks at a charge of £1 10*s* per insertion; total amount £78 net. (*Signed*) Epps & Co., Curecine Works, Camberwell E.C.' – nothing being written on the order form as to terms of payment. Now Mr Publisher was delighted with the order and gave me a cheque at once and I walked out of the office richer by £19 19*s*. Several of my friends including the patentee were waiting for me at the appointed rendezvous and we soon melted the cheque and cut it up between us".

The author of the account claimed to have placed ads for E.C. with hundreds of country and London papers – with the help of fellow canvassers – until the genuine Epps of cocoa fame circularized the press disclaiming all connection with this lively rival, and refusing to advertise in any journal which carried the other's advertisements. By this time, of course, it was too late – all the insertions were to run for a twelve month period. Orders for the medicine came rolling in, and the canvassers were to be seen in the company of the patentee rolling out of pubs all over London. In due course the "firm" came to grief, "not having paid for even one advertisement."

The activities of the "publishers of obscure directories", something of a scandal in Britain in recent years, were also familiar to the Victorians. Variations were played on the theme, and there was no limit to the enterprise and audacity of the unscrupulous. One of the best names in directory publishing was that of the American firm, Appletons, known for its European guides and hotel trades directories. One fine day the city of Birmingham was visited by two elegantly attired American canvassers representing Appletons. Naturally enough, they took a suite in the city's leading hotel and were to be seen riding about the city in a luxury brougham – hired. They were prepared to take orders for inserts in the Appleton directories, which they ostentatiously carried about with them, but only for cash down. This method of conducting business was common enough, and no one dreamed of questioning the integrity of an Appleton agent. As a result the two imposters were able to collect orders to the tune of £7,000 in a month. And then they left.

Nineteenth century advertisers made use of media that form no part of the publicity man's franchise today. Lengthy extracts from publishers' catalogues, for example, were once included in the end matter of books; today however – except for some paperbacks – such publicity has withered away to a few titles listed on the dust jacket. Book publishers also issued many periodicals of general interest (now the province of newspaper groups and specialist magazine companies) and liberally filled their pages with house ads. And it was the general book publisher who pioneered the part work, in which manufacturers advertised.

In nineteenth century London the advertiser was at work, not only in the pages of the part work, but also on bus and tram tickets. A passenger on the London Road Car Company in the 1890s would find himself admonished to "marry a plain girl if she uses *SOPOLIO*"; and on the tickets of the London General Omnibus Company to use Mr Harness' Electropathic Belt. Some advertisers exploited this novel medium to offer special terms on their goods that were the more compelling since the prospective customer was actually being carried to the shop, by the advertisement so to speak. The balding traveller bound for High Holborn might well make time to visit No. 95 where he was promised a twenty-five per cent discount on a large bottle of Edwards' Harlene. Passengers using the services down New Oxford Street were tempted to break their journey at Henry Glave's shop where they were promised the refund of their fare on any purchases amounting to more than three shillings. Arthur J. Hicks, of Craven House, London, announced: "£200 given away each year for collecting these tickets", while for the sporting enthusiast a three penny ticket meant a fifty per cent discount on the entrance fee to the Central Skating Rink, High Holborn.

The tram or bus ticket became such a well established medium that other bodies issued advertisements in the form of these tickets. It was a favourite of the evangelical religious sects who distributed "fares" for: Free Excursions from the City of Destruction to the Celestial City; the Direct Route from Death to Life *via* The Cross; and, on the Salvation Railway, from Sin-Land to Glory-Land "where they shall praise the Lamb for ever", Revelation 22.v. In the same way, estate agents offered plots of land, The Singer Company promoted its sewing machines, and the *Daily News* promoted its sales, while at least one candidate for Parliament promoted himself. In the general election of January 1906, the electors of Ashton-under-Lyne were handed free first class rail tickets which on closer inspection proved to be a "return for G. Algernon Moering to Westminster by a great majority".

2
THE BIRTH OF THE AGENCIES

The advertising agency is so much a part of contemporary society that it is easy to overlook its long history. Starting with the "classified advertising order offices" of the late eighteenth century it has grown into the complex service organization that we know today. A surprising number of modern London agencies have their roots in the nineteenth century; one even dates back to 1837, the first year of Victoria's reign. As we might expect the pioneers were men of diverse origins – one a bookseller, another a printer, another a coffee shop proprietor. But while many sprang from old and respected trades, others were disreputable operators willing to turn a quick penny by any method. The Victorian business communities had an in-built aversion to advertising as such. One can understand why agents had an uphill struggle to establish their good standing. Sometimes, indeed, they themselves concurred in the contemptuous verdict of society at large. Grace Brothers of Bristol rejected the title of "advertising agents"; their managing director replied to a journalist's question: "Friend, we are not advertising agents; though we do give out our esteemed friend Fry's cocoa announcements."

Yet even from the beginning the fraternity of agents did have "respectable" connections. James White, under whose son Robert, Whites became a true advertising agency and is now the oldest London agency still in existence, was a friend of the essayist Charles Lamb and even obtained "copy" from him. Born in 1775, White was educated at Christ's Hospital where he was a contemporary of Lamb. From 1800 he combined his job in the Treasurer's office of his old school with that of "agent for provincial newspapers", and also took a hand in promoting the state lottery. It was in this latter connection that Lamb helped him. We find the essayist's sister writing to Mrs Hazlitt. "James has got Charles to come down and write more lottery puffs." When James White died in 1820, the agency business was continued by his widow, and from 1831 by their son Robert Faulder White. Under Robert it finally lost its provincial newspaper slant and became an advertising agency in the usual sense of the word.

Design and studio services, so much a part of modern agency work, were still a thing of the future. A late Victorian agency had other selling points. First, it could offer a London advertiser easy access to the provincial press. Before the coming of the mass circulation national newspapers, a nationwide campaign implied the provincial as well as the London papers. But there were hundreds of local papers, unfamiliar to the London businessman, and difficult for him to track down and co-ordinate. Since the 1700s certain agencies had supplied provincial editors with London and foreign news. The London offices of these firms became the natural starting place for a survey of the resources of the provincial press. They made it their business to supply information on advertising rates, and then to place the advertisements for the London firms. One of the most famous of all such agencies was Taylor's. At his office in the Strand, clients could glance through copies of the leading provincial papers to assess their media value. From the 1780s Taylor was placing advertisements all over England. File copies of local papers exist with names written across the advertisements as a record of who placed them – Taylor's name occurs again and again. This liaison between London and the provinces was one of the main functions of an early advertising agency.

The early history of Street Brothers illustrates another service they had to offer. Streets proudly trace their origins back to a London newsagents and booksellers business owned by the first George Street. It is known to have existed as early as 1818 at an address in Serle Street on the site of the present Land Registry Office. Soon after this date George Street took the job of advertisement clerk with *The Times*, apparently leaving the family business to be run by his sons – Sam, Probert, George, Arthur and Edmund. Street Brothers seem to have started business as advertising agents by advancing credit to would-be advertisers. At this time *The Times* would allow neither credit nor discounts to advertisers, and paid no commission to people who brought advertising business to the paper. However, *The Times* must have soon realized that the connection with Street Brothers was a valuable one, because it soon began to pay them a quarterly retainer. When George Street died, his five sons continued to develop the advertising side of the business almost to the exclusion of the original book trade and newsagency. After a few years George and Edmund set up business on their own as G. Street & Company, with offices at 30 Cornhill, London. George seems to have been the most dynamic of the brothers. His new company overtook the old family concern, expanding into the field of foreign advertising, and developing interests in shipping and exports. Like any successful Victorian advertising agent, he published his own directories. One of his first publishing ventures was the *Indian and Colonial Mercantile Directory*, which reflected the firm's overseas speciality. By the 1870s the company had become so successful that George Street not only extended the premises in Cornhill, but also had the façade entirely redesigned by his elder brother William, who was now a successful architect. William was also commissioned to redesign the office interiors, although the result would not have won any prizes from the Council for Industrial Design. The working conditions seem to have been a little too much at times even for a clerk of a hundred years ago; the door to the basement, where the files were kept, was adorned by a skull and crossbones and the legend: "Abandon hope all ye who enter here!" In 1874 the company came under the control of new partners when Edmund and his friend George Jackson bought out the older George Street. In 1900, the company re-amalgamated with the founder company of Street Brothers.

By a time honoured convention observed among the select band of writers of histories of advertising, the town crier has a secure place in the story. His paragraph tends to fall in the extensive but thinly populated territory between the wall posters of Pompeii and the funnies of *Addison's Spectator*. It is true that the crier had an important function in town affairs before the advance of literacy displaced him by the printed poster. But his business was largely restricted to official announcements with the occasional "lost and found" thrown in. As his importance as a public functionary waned, however, he seems to have been willing to call the wares of any tradesman for a fee, and in this respect he has a place in the history of the advertising agent. From the Midlands, at the end of the nineteenth century, come two examples of this transition from crier to agent. E. Irons and Son, of 29 Park Square, Luton, Bedfordshire, described themselves as "Town Criers and Bill Posters". In the nearby town of Bedford Mr Stock – "advertising agent, bill poster and

Crier" – was still to be seen in the streets. "Of portly and handsome presence, the old gentleman, dressed in a grandly laced scarlet coat and knee breaches and cocked hat to match ambles about the town on his daily rounds," said the local paper.

The crier may still have served a useful purpose in the smaller towns, but in the cities he had long been a figure of the past. In London news was disseminated by the daily press, directories, and business publications of all sorts. Gossip and all the news not fit to print went the rounds at the coffee houses, which occupied a central place in the commercial life of the capital from the mid-seventeenth to the mid-nineteenth century. Lloyds, the greatest underwriters in the modern world, had its origins in the coffee house opened in the City of London in 1691 by Edward Lloyd of Lombard Street, "a few doors from the General Post Office". But Lloyds was just one among more than 2,000 known to have flourished during the two centuries of the coffee houses' greatness. Businessmen of all kinds used them as reading rooms, clubs, and exchanges, and the proprietors of the more popular houses stocked not only the London dailies but also the leading provincial and foreign newspapers, and kept them on file. Some were willing to take advertisements on behalf of the papers. In the 1770s, for example, we find the Rainbow Coffee House in Cornhill acting for the *Morning Post and Daily Advertising Pamphlet.* At least one proprietor actually became a fully fledged advertising agent. Mr Samuel Deacon opened his coffee house at No. 3 Walbrook, near London's Mansion House in 1822. By 1838 he was listed in the trades directories as a coffee house and keeper, and "Agent for the Country newspapers". Nine years later, an advertisement in Mitchell's *Newspaper Press Directory* shows that Deacon's business activities had expanded, for clients wishing to place advertisements in London or country newspapers were now referred to S. Deacon's office in 21 Walbrook. In fact these activitics continued to expand so that in 1863 Deacons began publishing their own directory.

Directories like Deacon's grew out of the broadsheet lists of newspapers that newspaper agents began publishing in the 1820s and 1830s. But most of these broadsheets were misleading and some were wilfully deceptive. The really absurd claims as to circulation came later in the century, but publishers were always willing to give themselves the benefit of the doubt. The sheets themselves were far from scrupulous. Rather than laboriously check facts, they cheerfully listed journals long since out of print, or omitted others that did exist. Perhaps the omissions were not so careless, though, for we must remember that the agent putting out the sheet would have arrangements with some newspapers and not with others. It is not hard to guess which would be omitted. One of the more reliable of these sheets was published by Lewis & Lowe, "British Foreign and Colonial advertisers and newspaper agents". At some point in the planning of their third issue they decided to do the job properly; the result was a little book which appeared in 1844, and which is probably the first serious attempt at a directory of the British press. This *Advertiser's Guide to the Newspaper Press of the United Kingdom*, price one shilling, was a thirty-six page octavo booklet which showed the average circulation, average number of advertisements, the political character, and the price, of each paper. An important function of these early lists was that of catalogue. Most agents were also newsagents – newspaper sellers – and issued lists to advertise their stock; hence the need to give the prices of the journals. More interesting is the directory's attempt to give some guide on circulation. The figures were based on the tax stamps for each paper. Although rough and ready, this guide at least gave some protection against publishers' inflated claims. The idea of introducing the average number of advertisements as a statistic was advanced, but it did not catch on in later directories. No doubt it gave advertisers some idea of the relative success of different newspapers, but it can hardly have been popular with the publishers who after all financed the agents.

In the 1840s there was still only a handful of agents. Indeed, the trade of advertising agent had barely emerged from the newspaper agents and coffee shops where it was born. That it did emerge, and establish itself as a new profession, was due largely to Charles Mitchell. A Manchester man, Mitchell had begun his career as an apprentice in the offices of the *Manchester Courier* and had then been promoted as their London agent. In this job, he had to collect accounts from old advertisers, and recruit new ones. In the last decade before the railways, he had to make frequent and arduous journeys on the London – Manchester mail coach. Most of the newspapers published outside London – they were few – had no London offices, and so had to have some such cumbersome arrangement, or seek the help of one of the few London newspaper agents. But things left much to be desired; anyone who could bring organization into this haphazard set-up had a bright future. Mitchell had plenty of opportunity to find out what was needed, and during the next twenty years he was to provide it.

When Mitchell set up shop as a "Town and Country Advertising Agent" in Red Lion Court, London, in 1836, a crucial episode in advertising history had begun. There was nothing revolutionary in his methods. What was new was the thoroughness with which he applied them, and the ambitious notions he had about his professional status. The few agents in business in the 1830s did little more than place advertisements in the provincial press for London businessmen, and provide them with a reading room in which they could study the papers published outside London. Mitchell offered an additional service of special interest to publishers and authors, and apparently it was very popular: making use of his regular contacts with country editors he undertook to send out review copies of books, prints and music, together with the advertisements for them. But more important than this was Mitchell's busy development of new publicity techniques. Among other things he built up two specialist mailing lists. The first of these "directories" covered reading rooms, literary societies, exchanges and commercial rooms, collegiate and public libraries, mechanics' institutes and book clubs. It had presumably been developed as part of his promotion work for the book publishers. The other list was described as a directory of all the public and private schools with the names of the principal teachers or the proprietors.

Like most businessmen of the day, Mitchell lived over his premises in Red Lion Court. He did not move out to the residential suburbs until 1847, when he was already in his late forties. It was no part of his plan to spend valuable time each day travelling to and from work; there was too much to be done. For besides being an agent, Mitchell also ran a small publishing house, and although most of his books were of family or domestic interest, he also published all the principal plays that came to London. Indeed, Mitchell cut quite a figure in London's literary world. He numbered Dickens among his friends, and met the Hungarian patriot and revolutionary journalist Louis Kossuth, for whom he arranged a job on the *Atlas* newspaper.

Nothing could show more clearly the prestige that Mitchell came to enjoy than the remarkable presentation made to him at the Guildhall on 24 March 1851, his birthday. At a cost of £170 to themselves, some 200 editors, proprietors and authors subscribed to the purchase of a "tea and coffee equipage" in silver, weighing 270 ounces. Few businessmen in the history of commerce can surely have received such a princely gift from their customers.

Apparently Mitchell had no sons of his own, and in the 1840s he began to train his stepson Walter Wellsman in the business. The young man took over much sooner than could have been expected, for his stepfather died in

February 1859, from injuries sustained in a railway accident the previous year. For some years Wellsman had been acting as sub-editor on the firm's famous *Directory*, and in 1859 he took over the editorship. He at once extended the scope of the work by including a directory of magazines and periodicals. In later years he added the main Continental papers (1877), the principal publications of the United States and Canada (1880), the press of Australia and New Zealand (1885) and in the following year India and South Africa.

The *Newspaper Press Directory* was the coping stone of Charles Mitchell's achievement. When the first edition appeared in 1846 it claimed, if wrongly, to be the first of its kind ever attempted. Not only were there many broadsheet lists of newspapers on the market, but the little booklet of Lewis & Lowe could stake a reasonable claim to comprehensiveness. What was new about Mitchell's book was its thoroughness and detail. The *Advertisers' Guide* was essentially a list, although its statistical information was valuable and, in the matter of circulation figures, not matched by Mitchell's *Directory*. But the latter contained a large descriptive section, and interesting and valuable introductory chapters on basic themes of advertising.

The *Directory* was dedicated to "the conductors and proprietors of the Public Press the true and enlightened promoters of knowledge". It takes the form of an octavo hardback book, 474 pages in extent, and contains a list of every newspaper and journal published in Great Britain and Ireland, with a description of their political affiliation, field of interest, area of circulation, address, price and other information so as to "promote the interests of the proprietors and form a guide for advertisers in their selection of journals as mediums more particularly suitable for their announcements". Mitchell does not go into the question of circulations but in the large section given over to the trade advertisements some of the journals make the ambitious claims usual at that time. In addition to the *Directory* proper and the advertisement section there were a number of short editorial chapters which formed a major feature of the publication in future years.

Mitchell's importance in the development of advertising as a profession is clear in the chapter headed "The Legal Position and Relation of the Advertising Agent". London offices that placed advertisements in the provincial press were not new, yet all but the largest were regarded with suspicion both by the newspaper proprietors and by the advertisers. At best, each party regarded him as an agent for the other. At worst, he was looked on as an untrustworthy parasite on the business community. Mitchell set about building up a respectable reputation for himself and his colleagues with determination and a proper Victorian sense of dignity. He argued that, whatever his reputation among the business fraternity, the advertising agent was indispensable. "Without him it would be impossible to carry on the provincial newspapers." This seemed a large claim, but it was not far from the truth. In the days before massive national circulations the manufacturer had to use the provincial press if he wanted to mount a national campaign. Yet the business of inserting a single simple ad could involve him in separate business transactions with a hundred or more editorial offices, even supposing that he knew how to locate the best media for his purposes. The convenience of a London office, where the major provincial papers could be studied and an advertisement placed for multiple insertion, was obvious. There were benefits for the newspaper, too, in an age when many businessmen looked upon advertising as an expense that did not need to be paid for. An agent saved the proprietor the trouble of checking on the credit, solvency and reliability of each new advertiser who applied for space in his columns. He also saved him the trouble of multiple business transactions. Finally, of course, an advertising agency which worked for several newspapers saved each of them the cost of keeping a full time "collecting clerk" in town to receive the payments of the advertisers. As we have seen, this was the very job from which Charles Mitchell launched his own career.

Most of Mitchell's readers would have accepted, however grudgingly, that the advertising agent was necessary; but they still distrusted the breed. The manufacturers' main fear, which was to last in one form or another to the end of the century, was that the agent simply represented the newspapers, placing ads only in those which gave him the best commission. There were indeed plenty of sharks in the advertising business, but Mitchell was not one of them. He was determined that the profession as a whole should not suffer because of them. As he saw it, the hub of the problem lay in the very word "agent", and this is where he attacked. An advertising agent was called an agent simply because hardly any other name could be ascribed to him, but "the meaning of the phrase is simply that he *carries on the business of advertising*", not that he acts for someone else. As the main function of a reputable agent was to offer the advertiser advice on the media available, and to select those best suited for his purpose, he could not possibly be the *agent for* any specific newspaper or group of papers since an "agent does not select his principal". This was exactly what advertisers feared – that while appearing to "select" for their benefit, the agent in fact recommended the papers that he was acting for. There was no real way round this "credibility gap" except a leap of faith. It is a measure of Mitchell's integrity that he convinced his advertisers of his fair dealing. But if the advertising agent could not act for the newspapers, no more could he act for the advertisers. If he did, not he, but the advertisers would be responsible for the transaction, and the chief value of the agent to the newspapers would be lost. The result of all this was important for the future – the advertising agent is a principal in his own independent line of business. It was the first real milestone on the road of respectability.

Mitchell's *Newspaper Press Directory* continued to come out until 1856, although not at the planned yearly intervals, and the editor again promised to make it an annual publication. In 1854 it had changed its format for a larger page size, gone into paperback, and cut its price to two shillings. These changes were the result of new ideas on layout and design, rather than of any loss of popularity. In fact the *Directory* continued to be a standard guide to the end of the century. As far as Mitchell at least was concerned, the popular response justified his description of his brain child as a "NATIONAL WORK", and he capitalized on this popularity in the introduction for 1856 to increase his domination of the market. "It is highly desirable," he wrote, "that the prospectus of every new newspaper and the first copy should be forwarded to Mr Charles Mitchell, the publisher of the *Newspaper Press Directory*, in order that they may not be omitted in the descriptive part of that now recognized work." This descriptive part was still the best thing of its kind on the market, but the editor also extended the scope of the features. In the second year he included an article on the laws of libel as relating to newspapers, "written expressly for this work by a special pleader (lawyer)", as well as the brief history of the newspaper, the piece on the advertising agent, and an article describing the London and country press. In 1856 these were supplemented by an article dealing with the changes in the law relating to newspaper taxes; and by a highly instructive little essay entitled "The Philosophy of Advertising". This dealt with three basic principles of a fast developing art: the techniques of copy writing, the question of circulation quality and quantity, and market analysis.

In his first issue Mitchell had made good the advertising agents' claims to be a professional body. A decade later he advanced in another direction. "Advertising is an art as well as a trade. There is an art in writing an advertisement."

Mitchell's comments were brief but to the point. Copywriters should avoid being verbose or turgid, but this did not mean that anything would do so long as it was only short and pithy. There was no general rule. The secret was to think about the product, make a decision about its main selling points, and then highlight them. Maybe in the end a longish piece of copy would be needed; if so the writer must inject some suspense – to draw the reader into the paragraph without revealing everything at once. In this aspect it appears French advertisements were far ahead of their English counterparts. The next generation of agents were to campaign for the control of copywriting; Mitchell is content to offer advice to advertisers on how to improve their own pitch. Nevertheless the idea was growing that the business required a special expertise, and from that it was a short step to the arrival of the experts.

Mitchell deals next with the selection of the media, traditionally the field in which the agent had most to offer. Here there were three things that had to be considered: "the classes to whom they are addressed, the towns in which they circulate, and the interests they advocate". First, numbers are not everything when it comes to evaluating a circulation. Over the next fifty years many a long battle was to be fought over circulation figures. But, at least, if the advertiser could not trust a thing the publisher claimed, he could occasionally disregard it entirely. For a start, "Some of the most widely circulated journals are valueless for the advertiser because their readers make few purchases." Blunt perhaps, but it does state the assumption underlying all systems of readership analysis. Mitchell expatiates: "A journal that circulates amongst the families of the district – one which has the confidence of the moneyed classes and respectable of society – one which from its character is likely to be read attentively by its circle of readers in their own homes and at their own firesides, and which finds access to news rooms and libraries, is better with a circulation of 2,000 than another of 4,000, that circulation being chiefly confined to inns, public houses and beer shops." But here the argument develops an unexpected logic. It is not so much a matter of money – though we can assume that those who frequent beer shops have less of it. The point is rather that people reading at leisure are more likely to browse through the ads and refer back to them. In marked contradistinction, public house readers were interested only in the latest news.

Next Mitchell discussed geographical coverage. Straightforward enough, perhaps, but he had an interesting point to make which brings the England of his day to life for us in a vivid way. He is arguing against the idea, apparently gaining ground in the 1850s, that with the coming of the railways and the increasing national coverage offered by the London dailies, it was enough to use these only. Not so, says Mitchell. A London paper read in the provinces is not the same as that paper being read in the City or the East End. In the first place its price makes it something of a luxury. In many cases single copies are bought by reading clubs with a dozen or so members. They are read hurriedly and passed on to the next member; there is no time to browse through the ads. Even where the paper belongs to one individual he will hurry past the advertisements of a London paper, assuming that they are intended for the London market only. So, despite fast railway deliveries, the provincial papers were still the best way to reach the provinces in 1856. Such at least was the view of one man, much of whose income derived from placing ads in the provincial press. Lastly, Mitchell has a few words to say on the subject of readership. It would be useless, for example, to address the aristocracy through the *Sunday Times*, the clergy through the *Globe*, or the moneyed interest through the *Morning Post*. His analysis is extended to cover a number of other London newspapers, and the result is a handy guide to the main media of the mid-nineteenth century.

All the essays we have been looking at are short, and the topics they touched on were to be dealt with with increasing refinement as the advertising art evolved. But taken together they constitute the first serious document of English advertising theory, and incidentally give Charles Mitchell a good claim to be considered the pioneer of modern advertising in Britain. Mitchell died before things really began to move, but there were plenty of signs of what was to come. An old newspaper proprietor quoted in the *Directory* of 1856 had some "kind comments" to make which were also to the point. "Of late years advertising has increased and is increasing. The 'advertising agent' has become much more of a man of business than he was formerly. . . . It will be important in the future that only men of honour and integrity be recognized by proprietors. . . . Such men cannot be too highly appreciated; they are poorly appreciated in a pecuniary sense." Victorian advertisers would not be the only ones to agree with such sterling sentiments. In the decades that followed, however, there were many agents willing to forget integrity if the money was good. But after Mitchell they would be looked on as black sheep in an otherwise honourable profession.

3
A NEW PROFESSIONALISM: THE AGENCIES DEVELOP

In an interview published in an English Sunday newspaper in November 1970, Professor J. K. Galbraith of Harvard University observed: "The goal in this world is not consumption but the use and enjoyment of life." The quotation was chosen by the editor to headline the story. No doubt it seemed to him in some way a striking, possibly even controversial, phrase. With characteristic blunt elegance Galbraith simply expressed what many people had long been thinking, and may soon be acting on. He was commenting on "the modern idea that the pursuit of wealth can be carried out, and its conditions studied, without direct or conscious reference to the other sides of human or social life". These, however, are the words of William Cunningham in his book *The Growth of English Industry and Commerce* published in 1882. Like Professor Galbraith, Cunningham was drawing attention to a process that was already familiar to his readers, and like Galbraith he had something to say about the role of advertising.

Somewhat surprisingly he saw in it a threat to private enterprise. "There are many ways in which the capitalist is compelled to go to great expense if he wishes to hold his own against his rivals. . . . Such for example are the enormous expenses of advertising to which manufacturers are put and the waste from exposing their goods and decorating their (shop) fronts, which affects the profits of many retail dealers; owing to expenses of this kind which their system enables them to avoid, the great Cooperative stores undersell the ordinary London retailers. Private enterprise can no longer provide the best channels for the distribution of wares." Perhaps a little out-of-date even in his own day, Cunningham saw the business of the trader in simple terms – to supply quality goods at a fair price in the belief that good wine needs no bush. Recognizing the power as well as the expense of effective advertising, he believed that the small family business – for him what the term "private enterprise" meant – was doomed to extinction. The future, he thought, belonged to large units such as the Cooperative Wholesale Society, or the Army and Navy Stores (originally a discount house for members of the forces), which aimed to cut out the retailer in favour of their own client-members. William Cunningham may have looked on advertising as a regrettable and distracting burden laid on the honourable trader by the pressures of the mass consumer society; but some of his contemporaries had already developed more advanced attitudes on the subject of marketing. The author of *An Advertiser's Guide to Publicity* (1887) set out the principle that still underlies our product oriented society: "The usefulness and value of most things depend, not so much upon their own nature as *upon the number of people who can be persuaded to desire and use them.*" The italics are in the original. The anonymous writer would undoubtedly have agreed with Galbraith's dictum: "Advertising exists by persuading people to consume." He might however have been surprised to hear that such old ideas were still being peddled in the 1970s as though they were novelties.

The *Advertiser's Guide*, which will repay further study, was itself a piece of publicity material. Published by Moody's Printing Works, 10 Dale End, Birmingham, it is a thirty-two page booklet containing practical observations on how to set about the business of advertising. It ends with a recommendation to the reader to try the services of Moody's Advertising, which existed to "design advertisements and to insert them upon the most advantageous terms, in any newspaper in the world".

The plan of the little treatise is straightforward; the main text is introduced by some comments on the value and antecedents of advertising, and the conclusion consists of a number of favourable quotations from eminent and not so eminent people. The writer is anxious to stress the respectability and value of his profession. The hoardings of Messrs Willings, he thought, "afforded a better education to the street Arab than many of the schools". Then follows the testimony of the *Manufacturers' Gazette*, which incidentally not only provides a worthy buttress to the writer's argument, but is also very interesting in its own right: "The history of the successful businessmen in this country is so pregnant with tributes to the power of advertising that the first attempt at a collection of biographical sketches in the world of business was made by a firm entirely devoted to the profession of securing advertisements and having the same published." Had the "firm entirely devoted to the profession" written this piece of copy we would not today be wondering who they were. Still, the point has been made: advertising can make men rich. What more telling tribute can there be than that?

Yet, in Moody's view the wise man, once he has made his fortune, looks to his reputation, and particularly his standing with posterity. Just as the merchant princes of Renaissance Italy had transmitted their names to future generations through their patronage of literature, so, it appeared, the great business houses of Victorian England would keep their names green in the memory of a grateful posterity by their patronage of talent in poetry and the arts. Renaissance patronage certainly had a large element of prestige for public relations in it, but few would agree that such engravings as *Health crowning Beauty* commissioned by Beecham Pills entitled that company to a reputation as enlightened patrons. Nor, in his heart of hearts, does Moody for he admits that "neither beauty nor utility has, as yet, taken any prominent part in the art of advertising". In view of all this it is not quite clear whether we are to regard the poet laureate as one of advertising's more illustrious progenitors, or merely as an over-rated scribbler. "What was the poet laureate," observes *The Advertisers' Guide to Publicity*, "but a man of ability who was retained to write advertisements?"

After his ambitious but confused opening the author gets down to cases, and we soon learn that he knows his stuff. The fact that Moody's emphasized their willingness to design advertisements is in any case significant, and points to the developing awareness of this major factor in successful publicity. The booklet quotes the American advertising agent George P. Rowell to support its contention, and he puts the case neatly enough: "A well laid out advertisement is never sleepy, lazy or unproductive but, on the contrary, it frequently creates want, as well as tells people where such can be supplied."

But an important rider is added by our anonymous writer: "Originality is the peculiar genius of the advertiser's art . . . and when novelty wears off the power has departed even if the thing still serves as a finger post or directory." Moody's naturally emphasized the importance of good design since it was one of the special services that they were themselves offering, yet the advice was still good. In the 1880s advertising was gradually becoming too specialized a field for managers or manufacturers to dabble in.

But Moody's had something further to offer in addition to skilled design – something we would now call "public relations". For "in new discoveries sufficiently important to demand the attention of journalists, an agent can often find means to induce editors, lecturers and others to create an interest by special notices". With the decline in vogue of the public lecture the advertisers of today have lost one medium apparently available to their Victorian predecessors, but the practice of providing editorial offices with a ready-made copy promoting a given product, is now so general as to be hardly worth notice. To judge from the number of ads in the Victorian press that quoted enthusiastic testimonials from the editorial pages of newspapers and journals, the idea could not have been unfamiliar to Moody's readers. But the idea that an agent could actually place stories and awake editorial interest was clearly still rather a novel one.

Moody's stressed the value of newspapers and periodicals for a second reason, "for people think more highly of what they pay for than a gratis sheet". This principle, so exactly in tune with the Victorians' belief in the virtues of paying one's way, is then applied further. Knowing that the average reader was liable to forget an advertisement as soon as he read it, the writer suggests an extra come-on in the form of a circular free on application. These were the days when a penny stamp was worth a penny, and "what a person invests a stamp to obtain is sure to receive attention".

The *Advertisers' Guide* has much to say about the importance of layout and design. The reader is warned that in trams, stations, carriages, hotels, coffee houses or public rooms, advertisements should be terse and striking and would usually require engravings (at which, of course, Moody's were particularly good). There is much common-sense advice, too, on copywriting. Those same ads in public rooms, arrestingly embellished with a Moody's engraving, should also be reinforced with terse and striking copy. Those who could afford it should take a whole column and lay out a series of short advertisements on single theme in "some fanciful form". But however little money he had to spend, the advertiser should remember two golden rules. First, concentrate on a single item, do not fill the space available with a complete inventory of one's stock. Secondly, be original; filling column after column with announcements, which "but for the difference in name and address are identical in language substance and form", is simply a waste of money for all concerned.

During the 1880s the air was thick with advice to English advertisers on how to succeed. Mostly it came from those agencies which like Moody's could afford to put out promotional literature. But while they did give certain practical information in their publications, the basic message was always the same – *advertise*. There were already English success stories to prove the value of heavy advertising in a society still new to the idea, and to back up the sensational stories coming out of America. Yet many English businessmen still regarded advertising either as beneath their dignity or as a waste of money. Equally misguided, as the agencies thought, were those who launched their company or product in a blaze of publicity and then after a year or so stopped advertising in the belief that they were now well enough known.

Such attitudes obviously needed to be changed if the prospects of the advertising industry were to realize their full potential. Like Moody's Printing Works many agencies issued pamphlets, while some published full scale annual handbooks, paid for by newspapers who wanted to advertise their rates and circulations. They carried facts and features on how to advertise, and cautionary tales and "amusing and entertaining engravings" driving home the message. Six plates, with accompanying text, depict the fate of "The Man Who Never Advertised". The auspicious opening day when, gold bags in hand he points smugly to the cheque for £5,000 donated by Father, is followed by months of "waiting for a customer"! This terrible tale of failure ends with our young hopeful reduced to ignominious bankruptcy and working "for a salary he would have disdained to offer his office manager in days gone by", in the firm of a man grown rich by advertising. Another picture puts the point more succinctly. The rich advertiser emerges from his bank carrying the money bags that spell *success*, and even a cheque book. In the gutter stands a down-at-heel sandwich man (none other than the Man Who Never Advertised) whose boards proclaim the achievements of Smiths Mutual Advertising Agency.

The agency men eagerly studied events in America, and they could see an ocean of unlimited possibilities opening out before them; but before they could launch a business, there had to be advertisers to earn them their ten per cent. At a time when the whole operation was much simpler, even the man who did advertise regularly might well do it himself, bypassing the agency, and asking the printer to set up his copy. Pictures were used haphazardly; they were included mainly to draw the reader's attention to the copy rather than to convey the message themselves. The idea that an advertisement required design or laying out was still new in the 1880s. Where pictures were used as signposts, the block would generally be bought from the old stock of some general supplier or from the printer himself. Indeed, different firms often used the same blocks; in at least one case two billiard table manufacturers advertised in the same magazine with the same picture.

But as the numbers of journals, magazines and newspapers of all kinds grew, the agencies made great play with the multiplicity of the media; they had a sound asset in their own expert knowledge of the varying rates, circulations, and categories of readership. Dixon's of Oxford Street, a highly successful firm, did test runs from time to time to gauge the effective response from various media, and offered this confidential information to clients. Most agents undertook to deal with replies to the advertisement if the client wished; others claimed to be able to guarantee good positions for clients' advertisements. Many offered a discount out of their own commission from the newspapers.

Some agencies bought space in bulk from the press at a ten per cent discount, and then let it to clients at the official standard rate; in many cases their clients shared in the discount on large orders. This practice, which seems to have been pretty widespread, could cause problems. One agent, Louis Collins, consistently refused to give a discount, claiming that the quality of his service merited top rates. However, so many of his competitors did offer discounts that he felt obliged to point out the dangers. In his *Advertiser's Guardian* he warned that agents were liable to commit professional suicide if they continued this cut-throat competition. He described the case of one advertiser, who after studying the rate card from a magazine decided to employ an agent; to his astonishment the agent quoted a lower rate than the magazine itself. Accordingly he wrote an incensed letter to the editor demanding an explanation. The editor's reaction was to withdraw the agent's commission; Collins feared that unless this stopped agents would soon find themselves without any commissions at all.

Collins published the first edition of the *Advertiser's Guardian* year book in

1885; it was some 250 pages long and bound in hard covers. About half of the book was taken up with articles and information, such as the page rates of the London and leading provincial papers; the rest was taken up by advertisements by the media. The whole thing, which must have been very profitable, makes fascinating reading today. Collins, who seems to have written every word of the copy himself, mixed straightforward advice with polemics against competitors, the media or even against clients with whom he had fallen out. The copy is interspersed with allegorical engravings having evocative titles such as – "The author humbly presenting his book to Truth and Beauty" – or "The author in valiant combat with the Editors of the Provincial Papers." In the 1887 issue Collins devoted close on twenty pages to a rambling tirade against the firm of Sir Joseph Pease, whom he accused of avoiding payments of several hundred pounds. It appears that Collins had booked space on Pease's behalf for months ahead in various papers. Sir Joseph or his successors then decided to abandon the campaign, and left Collins with quantities of unsold space on his hands. The story, which is regularly interrupted by digressions on classical or moralistic themes, had many ramifications and comes very close to libelling Pease. Clients, indeed, seem to have been rather casual in their dealings with agents; one unfortunate agent lost his fee for placing advertisements for winter clothing during the months of December and January which – as luck would have it – were unseasonably warm. The client, furious that nobody bought his goods, accused the agent of wasting his money, and refused to pay up.

But agency-client relations were not always so bad. Collins was able to collect a bad debt from a Sussex wine merchant through timely knowledge of Tudor history. The client had commissioned Collins to produce a brochure on champagne. When it came to settling the account, "There was some difference between us as to a matter of five guineas for extras in the nature of printing and other incidental expenses. The gentleman did not feel inclined to pay. Noticing he had taken as his motto Cardinal Wolsey's memorable advice to Thomas Cromwell, I reminded him of the fact and urged him that he should not only quote it but also act upon it, and 'Be just and fear not.' The result was that he not only wrote to thank me for pointing out the origin of his motto, but sent me his cheque for five pounds in clearance of the outstanding bill and, in addition, a case of wine." Perhaps the fact that the pamphlet elicited an order for sixty dozen bottles from a member of the nobility softened the client's heart.

On the principle that people paid attention to anything they spent money to obtain, Collins – like Moody and many other agents – was a great believer in the brochure sent only on request. He wrote such pamphlets to commission, and often sent out samples of his work to encourage commissions from new clients. It was a useful sideline for an agent willing to take the trouble, but Collins did not always get the new custom he hoped for. Rather aggrievedly he notes the reaction of a "north country firm" to whom he had sent specimens of his booklets on Champagne and Tobacco. Instead of an eager request for him to promote their own product, he received an icy reply from the director, who was much grieved to think so much talent should be bestowed on such subjects as drink and smoke. "And yet," said Collins, "I do only my best in the interests of my clients."

By the mid-1880s ideas as to what constituted the best interests of the client, and how the agent should serve them, were changing quickly. It was no longer enough simply to advise on media and insert the advertiser's copy on the best cash terms. Collins offered both to "draw up" the advertisement and to illustrate. In a rival year book, *Successful Advertising: Its secrets explained*, Thomas Smith carried a ten page section of specimen type faces, clearly numbered so that the client could specify what he required. Some manufacturers were becoming keenly aware of the impact a well designed notice could make, and hired agents to help them against indifferent editors. Why, they asked, were the goods of their competitor Bloggs advertised in the same paper – perhaps even on the same page – with capitals and bold Gothic type, while theirs resembled a paragraph from the news pages? The agent's answer to this was simple enough – hire me to represent your interests, and to prepare proper typographical instructions. Very soon the agent could claim a new client.

Before long, however, the client would find himself being pressed by the agent to yield on a more sensitive matter. While conceding that typography and illustration were best handled by the artistic expert, most businessmen felt that at least they knew how to write English, especially when it came to selling their own product. After all, they had been salesmen all their lives, and knew what they wanted to say and how to say it. Thomas Smith disagreed. One of the secrets of successful advertising, in his view, was to hire an expensive literary gentleman to write the copy. And, as he so reasonably observed, what business could afford that kind of luxury? Better by far to delegate the job to an agent who could call on the services of any number of such silver-tongued wordsmiths.

Yet, surprisingly perhaps, clients were not always eager to have their own deathless prose rewritten. The advertising partner of an Irish firm reacted vividly to proofs of his copy after it had been worked over by his agent, and wrote in what can only be called the *STRONGEST TERMS*. "He thinks," ran the letter, haughtily using the third person mode of address, "mind he *thinks*, that the wording and style of the advertisement you received *might, just possibly*, be *something* like what he and his partners required to be inserted, and might on an accidental occasion, when particular attention was drawn to it, attract the eye of some of the unwary public. He will now retire to his cottage by the sea and give his shattered nerves time to recover, and at the same time await the arrival of new proofs." However, the articulate Irishman was no match for his agent – the cool-headed Louis Collins. Collins smugly concludes the story: "Yet the advertisement in question was inserted, after all, in the way I suggested."

Following Mitchell's example most large agencies and some small, like Collins, issued their own "press guide" or "advertisers' guide". Among them were Street, F. L. May, Samuel Deacon, and Henry Sell. Probably the best known was Sell's *Dictionary of the World's Press*. Sell started business at 167 Fleet Street, in 1869, and after more than ten years' experience in advertising decided to launch his own directory. It appeared first in 1882 under the title *The Philosophy of Advertising*, and two years later was rechristened *Dictionary of the World's Press*. Sell compiled the *Dictionary* with impressive thoroughness. In addition to British newspapers, he listed journals published in every part of the known world, and undertook to place advertisements in any one of them.

Most of Sell's comments on advertising and the media follow on from what Mitchell had to say, but he does make one new and perceptive point on the subject. An experienced advertiser will know from what class or classes his patrons will come, and will know what newspapers will reach them. But in choosing a paper for advertising, he will also take into account how the tone of the editorial pages can influence the reader's mind, even while he is browsing through the advertisements. Sell finds proof of this in the "extraordinary success" of advertising in the much respected religious papers.

As well as making special contracts for long campaigns, and securing premium advertising space, Sell could offer his clients a wide range of other specialist services. Many of these were to become the stock in trade of the better agents as the century progressed. Sell was in constant communication with "gentlemen of literary ability" whom he engaged to write good copy in prose or verse. He was aware of the importance of design in modern advertising. He boasted a large staff of intelligent typographers, engravers and designers, who were specially trained for advertising work, and had a printing department that could set up an ad in the type faces and styles of most leading London papers.

The large agency made its money from two sources, as Sell explained. First it had the newspaper's commission for all the ads it secured for them; second it could profit from buying space in bulk at a discount for the "wholesale" purchaser and reselling it to the public at the official rate. "Thus it will be found," Sell concludes, "that nearly all the best spaces in newspapers and magazines are in the hands of the agents." Neither newspapers nor advertisers cared for the situation, and sometimes the advertising manager of a large newspaper would try to cut out the agents. When a long series of ads were placed by an agent for a large client firm, the newspaper would send its advertising manager round to the firm's offices to offer it the discount – on condition that it bypassed the agent. Such deals clearly benefited both newspaper and advertiser. But the agent had many more opportunities as middleman to capitalize on the situation and, as the careers of men like Mitchell, Sell and Thomas Smith show, the agency business was a growth area in late Victorian England and the fertile soil for many new companies.

Thomas Smith, the founder of Smith's Mutual Advertising Agency, was born of working class parents in Boston, Lincolnshire, and his first job was as a railway porter in the Great Northern Railway there. At the age of twenty-five, promotion took him to the company's head offices in London. For him this move to the capital meant a good deal more than a company promotion, and he entered his chosen field of publishing as soon as possible. Within a few years he became manager of a publishing company, and committed all his fortunes to it. To judge from his own comments later in life, this venture was a gamble from the outset, and in fact the company went bankrupt. For Smith, then in his mid thirties, the collapse was a disaster and his health broke down under the strain. He returned to Lincolnshire to recover; there he renewed his determination to break into the London business world. "Those were dark days; but the finger of Providence seemed to point to London and to Fleet Street, to a small unfurnished back room, and to advertising as a means of livelihood."

The small back room was numbers 9 and 10 St Brides Avenue, and determined to "build on past experience all along the line of life" Smith revived his contacts in the printing and publishing worlds. At this watershed in his career he was apparently helped by many loyal friends. Among them were the advertising agent J. H. Lile, who at the end of the century still ran one of London's smaller agencies. But Smith had ambitions for his Mutual Advertising Agency; during the first eighteen months, helped by letters and interviews arranged by his friends and the goodwill of clients, he expanded so successfully that he had to move to new premises, this time to Wine Office Court where a number of printers were among his neighbours. Six years later, in 1885, he moved again, this time to Fleet Street proper.

From the mid-1880s the expansion of the firm continued at speed. Smith extended his range as a publisher when he bought the religious weekly *Great Thoughts*. This became the basis of other publishing ventures, and a printing works was soon added. Success continued to shine on him and in 1897 he built a modern printing works at St Albans, Hertfordshire, which was to specialize in advertising work. The last of Smith's various ventures was, rather oddly, the Lincolnshire Feather Factory at Boston, his home town. In his early days as an agent he had handled the advertisements for the struggling journal *Christian Signal*. This soon died, but not before the Mutual Advertising Agency had run a test ad on "How to sell feather beds through the post" (*sic*). The outcome was that one of London's leading agents found himself proprietor of a prominent feather bed manufacturers. Smith himself valued this not only as a profitable enterprise, but because it had its roots in his native soil. As befitted a self-made man he remained proud of his origins. To celebrate the firm's twenty-first anniversary he took the whole company by special train from King's Cross to Boston. There they "proceeded to the Lincolnshire Feather Factory, where breakfast was served and to which were invited some of the old railway employees who had been Mr Smith's fellow servants years ago. . . . The party then proceeded to Skegness where the remainder of the day was pleasantly spent."

Smith's success is instructive. After his first failure he cast around for a line of business not too crowded with competitors; the relatively new field of advertising was ideal for his purpose. Showing a remarkably advanced view of industrial relations, he instituted a profit sharing scheme. He exercised his craft unremittingly. From the very first year of its foundation the agency had issued its own press guide, *Successful Advertising*, which began as a two page circular but which had grown to a 400 page book eight years later. In it, Smith preached the gospel of advertising, enunciating as a general rule that advertising should account for between twenty and thirty-three per cent of any company's budget. He devised methods of testing circulation claims, stressed the need for expert design and layout, and from very early on employed professional copy writers. For the year ending December 1885, his seventh, he recorded a turnover of £48,000 of which £37,000 was in billings in nearly 1,500 papers and journals. Multiplying that figure by ten will give a rough idea in modern values of the size of the business, only seven years after its founding.

Yet Smith's agency was not the biggest. The most likely candidate for that place at the turn of the century was T. B. Browne Ltd, the "Central London Agency". In 1900 its central London office, called by a contemporary the "great *camera obscura* of Queen Victoria Street", employed more than 200 people, and had branches in Glasgow, Manchester and Paris. The business had started in the late 1860s in an office in Finsbury Place, London. It was built up by the founder, and joined in 1875 by his brother C. A. G. Browne. Seven years later this brother left to join Sell's as managing director and then set up on his own account in 1895, taking many of his former accounts with him. He was a much smaller operator than T.B. who achieved a major expansion in the field of foreign and empire advertising, and made a special study of the South African market. The massive *A.B.C. Press Guide* first published by the agency in 1888, and dwarfing all its contemporaries, reflects this internationalism of outlook.

Browne's really profitable innovation seems to have been in another field which verged on product development. "He regarded it as part of his business as an agent to assist in opening up new markets and in the developing of old ones," and he was always willing to supply his clients with market information. Browne's did not simply wait for clients to come to them, they initiated creative campaigns in advance. More and more agents were coming to realize that the road to expansion lay in providing a fully comprehensive service. Thomas Dixon's Biogen studio is a good example of how far the trend was developing, and it was probably as one of the pioneers of this approach that the Central London Agency of T. B. Browne was able to build up its commanding position.

Dixon's Oxford Street agency in London was in fact the successor of the one founded by Louis Collins. We will end this study of some of the personalities in the world of advertising in nineteenth century London with a closer look at this strange figure. Born about 1850, the son of a poor clergyman, Collins came to London in his teens. By the age of twenty-one he had an office in Great Marlborough Street in the West End handling the advertisements of J. J. Cash of Coventry, and Pease's Cotton Mills in Darlington. Later he lost the Pease account and conducted a vendetta against the company in his *Advertiser's Guardian* which he began publishing from Wine Office Court in 1883. The first number, merely a two page leaflet, appeared in the May of that year and was characteristically subtitled: "For circulation among advertisers only, that Plagiarists may not avail themselves of the writer's labour." Harbouring a well developed sense of persecution, Collins was soon to give it free reign. But here we will take a look at some of the valuable services he performed for advertising. Chief among these was the exposure of the "country papers trick". This was to lead him to the law courts on a charge of libel, but he was triumphantly acquitted; the judge remarked that he left the court without a stain on his character and had moreover performed a real service for the advertising community.

Inflated circulation figures were the nub of the quarrel, but there was a twist. Relying on the London businessman's lack of knowledge about the provincial press, some publishers were producing their paper in two or three editions in which nothing differed but the names. By this means three separate advertising outlets were made to grow where only one grew before. In some cases the deception was helped by the good reputation of the parent paper. Collins insisted that the advertiser should concern himself only with verifiable circulation figures and "the class and standing of the readers"; but businessmen were often ready to take these on trust from a "reliable" journal. Naturally the circulation for the whole was quoted to an advertiser for any of the three, since an advertisement appeared in them all – whichever one it was placed in. Many advertisers who did not realize this could be persuaded to pay three insertion fees under the belief that now they commanded three times the circulation.

This led to the second, and what one might term the "basic", swindle. Although his announcement was bound to appear in all three, the advertiser only had to pay for an insertion in one. But not knowing that the media were identical most advertisers were attracted by the apparently generous discounts offered for a bulk order. Collins suggested various ways in which the malpractice could be detected; but what really incensed him was that some apparently reputable agents would cheerfully handle such publications at a profit. At first they accused him of exaggeration, which was easy enough in view of his high flown prose and obvious excitability; then they claimed to have been ignorant of what was going on; finally they were obliged to mend their ways.

A simpler version of the country papers trick, also exposed by Collins, was hit upon by a band of outright con-men, based in Gresham Street, London. They saw no reason to circulate "provincial papers" in the provinces at all if London advertisers could be sold space on the strength of sample copies alone. Accordingly they brought out a number of papers with "circulations" of only a few score – which was at least enough to show to all the interested advertisers – and sold space on the basis of imaginary circulation figures. A few copies were sometimes distributed locally, but advertisers would have been horrified to learn that the journals were virtually unheard of outside Gresham Street. The charlatans were forced to take Collins to court – and lost. In a way it is surprising that Collins was not the target for more law suits. With methodical bluntness he published a complete list of all the duplicated newspapers he had tracked down, together with the names of the agents who dealt with them. Apart from forcing these agents to change their ways, the list also revealed that even the established directories, such as those of Mitchell, May and Samuel Deacon, had been listing these dubious journals without question.

Despite, or even because of, this kind of crusading, Collins never became one of the big firms. In 1893 Collins himself was bought out by Thomas Dixon and retired to Boulogne where he apparently succumbed to paranoia. Under Dixon the agency continued to evolve and moved to new offices at 197 Oxford Street, where it developed a highly original speciality which brought it business – not only from large client firms such as Pears, Colmans and Players – but also from the Bartitusu School of Arms. For Dixon's had pioneered the Biogen which brought the moving picture to advertising. This apparatus consisted of hundreds of photographs mounted on a drum; the drum could be rotated by electricity or an air jet so that the pictures flicked past an eyepiece in rapid succession to give the illusion of movement. Dixon's urged the animated picture upon advertisers as one of the ways of "keeping up with the reputation of the present age for mobility". They boasted large studios, and had "at their command a large number of ladies and gentlemen, connected as may be imagined with the profession, who are skilled in the assuming of character and expression of emotion and are trained in the work of tableaux".

Under Dixon then, the agency kept well in the forefront of innovation. But he was proud of his association with Collins and his sturdy struggle with the provincial press. And he was right to be so, for by his pioneer efforts in this field Collins had made a valuable contribution to the interests of advertisers and the smaller agents.

4
PROMOTIONS AND PROMOTIONAL LITERATURE

Advertising stunts succeeded if they made a dramatic and preferably shocking impact, and were intended as a nine days' wonder. When the makers of Hudson's Soap sponsored a stage coach drive from London to York in 1881, they anticipated a sudden upsurge in sales during the week the service ran, and possibly a small long term increase in the towns and villages along the route. Certainly the event was sensational. More than a hundred horses were used on each trip, and the drivers covered 120 miles in twelve hours; there was a revival of interest in the coaching era in the 1880s, and good press coverage was assured. But the effect was not a lasting one. In this Chapter we shall look at promotions of a more permanent nature. These usually entailed the distribution of some kind of object or literature, or the making of a long term sales offer for several weeks or months.

A classic type of early promotion was the "free trial" pioneered by the sewing machine manufacturers in the 1850s and 1860s. Around 1870 they advanced further in this direction when the makers of the *Florence* model offered: "Should any purchaser be dissatisfied with it, to give in exchange any sewing machine of similar price known to the trade." But the two mainstays of this kind of advertising were the "giveaway" and the free leaflet. The give-away ranged from Free Railway Insurance, to a recipe book offered by Bird's

Custard in the 1880s, to calendars "in three separate coloured designs" offered by W. Sheppard, a family grocer of Cheam. But probably the most famous, not to say notorious promotion in the whole history of British advertising came from the use of Sir John Everett Millais' painting, *Bubbles*, by the manufacturers of Pears Soap.

In 1899 a brief but acrimonious debate took place on this very issue. The painting, completed in 1885, had been bought from Millais by Sir William Ingram for reproduction in the *Illustrated London News*. Here it was seen by T. J. Barratt of the Pears Company who saw in this pretty piece of sentimentalism a way of boosting his firm's share of the soap market. The first step was to ask the artist's permission to use it; the hurdle was successfully cleared and Ingram claimed that he never heard a "single word of remonstrance from the artist as to its use". But Millais' son had a different story to tell in his biography of his father. Apparently the artist was furious. "He protested strongly against this utilization of his art, but – knowing that he had no power to prevent their using the picture in any way they liked – he at last consented to look at the specimens. Their excellence somewhat assuaged his wrath; he admitted, as he was bound to do, that the work was admirably done, and, with an expression of his regret at the purpose to which it was to be turned, the interview ended."

The young J. G. Millais, at least, had strong views on the commercialization of what he looked on as one of his father's finest works, and was anxious to defend him from any suggestion that he had lacked the highmindedness proper in these matters. Some people claimed that the elder Millais had made no objections at all, and were ready to produce evidence to buttress their assertions. According to Barratt of Pears, Millais had been delighted with the quality of the reproduction, describing it as magnificent, which indeed it was. Furthermore, he was quite content for it to be used as an advertisement: "He was full of praise. Encouraged by his generous word, I spoke of the advantage which it was possible for the large advertiser to lend to Art – he could give a very much greater publicity to a good picture than it could receive by being hung on the walls of the Royal Academy. Sir John Millais with alacrity appreciated the idea, and when I stated the extreme difficulty experienced by those desirous of advertising by means of the Graphic Art, to induce men to paint pictures owing to the artist's fear for his reputation, Sir John, taking his pipe from his mouth, said, 'What . . . nonsense! I will paint as many pictures for advertisement as you like to give me commissions for, and I will write you a letter for publication marking my appreciation of the excellent way in which you have dealt with the picture.' "

Pears' case was apparently proved. But the young Millais, forced to admit that he had not attended the interview between his father and the advertisement manager, nevertheless returned to the attack: whatever Sir John Millais may have said in public, at home he had been furious. But the other side were every whit as tenacious. They were able, moreover, to recruit a telling letter from Mr Charles W. Deschamps who had been the honorary secretary for the British Art Section of the Paris Exhibition of 1889. "At Sir Frederick Leighton's request I called upon Sir John Millais to ask him if it would be agreeable to him that *Bubbles* should be one of the pictures representing him at that Exhibition, notwithstanding its having been used for advertising. His reply was very vigorous and strong. 'Nonsense, why not? It is an admirable reproduction and is a credit to Messrs Pears, and to my picture, which is a very good one.' "

Was it Millais – or perhaps Sir Frederick Leighton – who was appalled at the prospect of Britain's reputation in the fine arts being traduced by this talisman of hygiene? It does begin to appear as if Sir John, not uninterested in business matters himself, was about the only member of the art world genuinely indifferent to the "prostitution" of his art. Remembering the serious promise of his early career, perhaps he knew that *Bubbles* was fit for nothing else but advertising soap.

That Sir John Millais approved the use of *Bubbles* as an advertisement for Pears was claimed by the manufacturers, supported by the evidence. Perhaps he would not have approved it if he had known how it was later to be exploited, for the fine art reproduction that Pears had shown him was not the end of the story. It was followed by second rate versions in colour, appalling black and white engravings, and – final indignity – a jigsaw puzzle. Reduced to postcard size and distributed in a cellophane bag, the miniaturized masterpiece at last joined the ranks of the novelties that held the advertisers' imagination in thrall during the 1890s. These novelties came in all shapes and sizes and, save for a few pretty exceptions, in varying degrees of nastiness. Some were made to a manufacturer's specifications, but most were produced speculatively by printers. In most cases they were given away, and some were sold; yet however they were distributed they do seem to have been popular.

Among the favourite items were puzzles and optical illusions. The Maypole Soap Dye Company decorated the front of its trade card with the picture of a clown in a colourful doublet; to enjoy the "Optical Delusion" one had only to move the card and Pierrot's eyes would move. Pears had a somewhat more insistent message. The name "Pears" was shown in white, reversed out of a vivid red disc. If one stared at this for a few minutes and then focused on a red spot below the circle, the magical letters would appear of their own accord – this time in red. Such scientific tricks had a wide appeal, but puzzles could be more profitable. The makers of Brookes "Monkey" ("Won't-wash-hands") household soap offered to pay £500 if they themselves could not solve their "interesting problem". This involved moving eight counters, marked with the initials of the company, on a board so as to make a given sequence. The solution could be had, together with a large bar of soap free to any address, by sending six penny stamps to the Company.

Cheaper – and more fun – than such catchpenny tricks, were the pretty little press-out models that came with Sunlight or Price's Toilet Soap. These took the form of sailing ships or pleasure boats with such titles as *Ocean Queen* or *Fairy Barque*. They were embossed on heavy card so that they would stand up to give a three-dimensional effect. The makers of Owbridges Cough Mixture had a different line in such paper models – ladies standing in marble gateways, or a lifeguard in his sentry box. More fun was the Owbridge cardboard sailor boy who danced on a string, or the kazoo (comb and paper) from Beecham's Pills, just the thing to provide the music. And in the days of home entertainment manufacturers did not neglect music in their promotion campaigns.

Those depressed by the perversion of well-loved folk songs for profit can find a bitter-sweet consolation in the thought that, years before the television jingle arrived on its screen, the same sort of thing had already been done, even to the nursery rhyme. Who now remembers Maypole's little ditty of the 1880s:

Little Miss Muffet, sat on a tuffet,
Her dollies' clothes all in a heap.
Beside her a gray bowl
Of dye made with MAYPOLE,
In which she would soon let them steep.

There were many others, tricked out with gaily coloured pictures and presented in little albums, which are now forgotten. Fortunately, traditional folk and nursery songs are too strong to be smothered by their ephemeral message.

Hoping to cash in on the popularity of the drawing room ballad, Holloway's Pills went into the business of publishing sheet music. Favourites such as *The Dream of My Life* and *My Love for Ever and Aye*, available for half-a-crown or free on application to the manufacturers, had only the most discreet mentions of their real origins. On the back, for example, we find two hearts entwined with underneath the legend, "True lovers of health should use Holloway's Pills." Holloway's great rivals, Beecham's, soon entered the same line of country but with a rather more sophisticated approach. Disdaining the weak pun, and Holloway's back page reticence, they published the "Beecham's Music Portfolio" in which the Company's name appeared in bold type across the front cover of medleys such as *Banjo Praises*.

No one could object to a company which chose to turn music publisher and commission popular songs as a gesture of patronage. People could well have objected to the treatment meted out to traditional nursery rhymes, and many people did object to the corruption of the familiar "Good morning" greeting. Thanks to a highly successful advertising campaign it became impossible to use this mundane phrase without fear of the snap response, "Have you used Pears this morning?" In fact, the gimmick had been tried at least once before in the 1840s by Messrs Sawyers of the Kingston Toilet Saloon: "Good Morning!" – "Have you been to Sawyers?" But this never became a part of the national idiom. Sawyers were too small to carry it off. Still, besides infuriating many people at least it provided *Punch* with a joke. The scene is the dining room of a country house at breakfast time, the caption, "A Pardonable Lapse of Memory".

> HOSTESS. "Good Morning! Mr Robinson, I hope you slept well."
> ABSENT MINDED GUEST. "Good Morning! Have you used Pears this morning? Er, . . . Oh, Yes thank you! Very well."

We shall deal with the art of the copywriter more fully later on, and need only note in passing that the search for the catch phrase had long been a part of his job. In the field of promotional marketing – our chief concern in this Chapter – the "free gift" is apparently just as old. It is not known when this odd tautology was first coined but the idea that one could profit from giving things away was certainly part of commercial practice in the early 1800s.

One of the first instances the authors have found dates from 1837, the first year of Victoria's reign. In January that year appeared the two-page *The Milton Advertiser or Literary Cabinet* which was supplied *gratis* to the customers of the Milton Press, Chandos Street, whose proprietor was John Nichols. Despite its proud title, the *Advertiser* was really nothing more than glorified trade card and price list. The first page was occupied by a write up of the Milton Press, while the second carried the price list for tradesmen's shop cards, ranging in quality from plain through "extra superfine" to "Creswick's patent enamel". None of this is too remarkable, except for a special announcement:

A Splendid
NEW YEAR'S GIFT!
Gratis

Both the wording and style proclaim this an authentic if primitive specimen of the "free gift", although the object on offer might not today be the first choice for a sales drive: this was an engraving "executed in the manner of a beautiful miniature likeness of John Milton", which Nichols believed would be appreciated by any lady or gentleman as a New Year's gift. Similarly, at the launch of *Cassell's Magazine* in 1867, the publishers gave away a large engraving of the famous painting the *South Sea Bubble*. The early date of the Milton Press presentation – 1837 – gives it a special interest which the *Cassell's Magazine* offer lacks. By the 1860s it was fairly common in both England and France for publishers to give away the first issue of a magazine or a novel appearing in weekly parts; Cassell's were merely following an established practice. But neither of these examples show the "free gift" in its fully fledged form. Both have features of the manufacturer's sample, although since Milton's Press specialized in the printed word rather than pictorial material, the Milton engraving gets nearer to the essential quality of the give-away: which is that the gift has nothing to do with the manufacturer's main line of business. By the late 1880s, however, the genre reached maturity. Mellin's Baby Foods of Peckham were among the firms who took the final step. In 1888 the following announcement appeared on the back page of Cassell's publication *Abbeys, Cathedrals and Churches*:

> MARVELLOUS MODE OF ADVERTISING
> No doubt the majority of people who read the following startling offer will scarcely credit it, but nevertheless it is an absolute fact that a well-known manufacturer of an Infants' and Invalids' food is prepared to send free on application a genuine silver brooch, manufactured from a very pretty description – Apply at once to G. Mellin, Peckham.

The somewhat breathless tone of the offer reveals the pride of the innovator. Half a century had passed since the Milton Press had made its New Year presentation, and many changes had been rung on the theme since then. But with the announcement of Mellin's, the "Marvellous Mode of Advertising" had definitely come to stay. In the last decade of the century a young lady of Boston, Mass., was able to subsist entirely on the samples she received from food firms by offering her services as a commission agent.

In March 1862, customers of Messrs Johnson Bros., Grocers and Tea Dealers of 3 Lower Road, Islington, London, found an unexpected novelty presented with their household purchases. As Mr Johnson thanked them with his customary politeness he pressed into their hands the first number of *The Family Grocer*. This was a little journal which was offered entirely *gratis* to his more esteemed patrons and which, he assured them, they would find both informative and useful. To the citizens of this solidly respectable suburb, who firmly believed in the value of instructive literature, the project must have seemed eminently worthy. We can imagine the lady of the house settling down eagerly to a perusal of the little magazine, as her housekeeper unpacked the groceries.

The venture was especially interesting since Johnson's had only recently taken over the business from Mr Mundy who had made the shop the leading emporium of its kind in the district. Only time would tell whether the new management would maintain his high standards, but for the moment it was flattering to be classed among the group of privileged patrons, and to have one's goodwill courted in such a novel way. Yet, in scanning the eight pages of this first number, the lady customers may have been a shade disappointed by the local grocer's editorial policy. He promised that future issues would carry a series of features on the main goods of the grocery trade, their history and places of origin, and advice and warnings against possible forms of adulteration. But the first number had nothing of this. Instead the reader was offered a number of informative, yet essentially boring articles on current affairs and matters of academic interest. As well as a long analysis of the succession problem in the principality of Saxe-Coburg, following the death of Prince Albert, there was a full page of esoteric criticism on a recent scholarly reconstruction of the Mausoleum at Halicarnassus.

Messrs Johnson's venture seems to have folded after the third number issued in May 1862. It would be pleasant to think that the sales upturn claimed in their first editorial had accelerated so fast that they no longer had to woo patrons with dissertations on the classics, or gobbets of stale news. But perhaps public apathy was responsible. The Victorians took their reading seriously, but even a housewife prepared to read about the difficulties of the committee for the memorial to Prince Albert drew the line at a feature on a siege gun powered by town gas. Nor was the "Grocer's" proof-reading of the best. An entertaining little piece on the manufacture of crinoline springs in Sheffield somehow became mixed up with yet another report on that indefatigable committee for the Albert memorial. The results were sensational. The article under consideration was titled, "How vast is Crinoline". It ran to two paragraphs that followed one another thus: ". . . Sheffield's production is now running at 150 tons per annum. Already enough crinoline has been manufactured to encircle the globe again and again.

"A monolith of due size and beauty is found to be unobtainable, and on the recommendation of the four advisers, Her Majesty has abandoned that form of memorial." This odd conjunction might startle even the most inattentive ladies.

But one feels that the editor is being unduly smug when he says of another journal: "It will not surprise many readers to learn that the Literary Gazette is defunct." Ironically, we can trace no further record of the *Family Grocer* after this, its third issue. As a literary achievement it was third rate, and as an exercise in journalism it was a disaster; yet it recruited a few hopeful advertisers.

As well as the expected house ads for "Johnson's – the Noted Tea Establishment with the Largest Assortment of Italian Goods in Islington" – there are insertions from other local tradesmen. Not surprisingly there were no other grocers, but we find chandlers, shoemakers, hosiers, milliners and haberdashers well represented. And then there were Messrs J. and T. Hall, the butchers, who had troubles with other people's principles and could do little about it. Their ad in the first issue informs customers that no business would be done on Sundays; this may not seem particularly remarkable, but this was an age when many families had their Sunday lunch cooked by the local baker and when a butcher could expect a certain amount of trade from people looking for a belated Sunday joint. Hall and his family seem to have been models of Christian rectitude. But when one reads their advertisements in the third issue of the *Family Grocer* one begins to wonder; here the address has been amplified and now we read "Messrs H. & J. Hall, 7 Lower Road, Islington (Next to the Chapel)."

Perhaps these family grocers were too ambitious in their promotions, but they were certainly acting in the spirit of the times. Companies of all shapes and sizes produced their own newspapers and magazines, and many an enterprising publisher launched out with a sheet financed entirely from its advertising. Earlier examples were limited to the domestic market, but later on the interests of American tourists were catered for. The *Dictionary of Common Wants* – "supplied *gratis* to steamship companies, especially the transatlantic services and to hotels in America, Great Britain and Ireland" – was a case in point. In 1874 the first number of the *American Traveller* appeared; in a special note to advertisers its publishers explain that the paper is distributed among the cabin passengers of the incoming steamers: "The number of Americans who visit Europe has been steadily increasing from year to year, and the large sums of money they expend while on their travels become proverbial."

We can see just how ambitious the "free" press could be from the *Great Western Advertiser* which first appeared in January 1843. It claimed a large circulation among the higher income groups and was distributed free to public houses, news rooms, hotels, commercial houses, magistrates, clergy, local government officials, the gentry, medical men, and respectable tradesmen in the south west of England. Editorial coverage was generous on general and local news; railway and post office details; city affairs and agricultural news. All objectional advertisements were rigorously excluded, and politics were avoided. All this was common enough, for such ventures had been launched in the Midlands, Scotland and Ireland. But the distribution set for the *Great Western Advertiser* was quite remarkable. Each week 5,000 copies were printed and yet the publishers guaranteed a 9,000 weekly circulation. There was no trick in this: the copies were circulated twice. On publication day the copies were distributed in all major towns of the south west, and two days later collected up and redistributed in the rest of the region. The mind boggles at the thought of running such an operation, and at the confidence with which the publishers allowed for a wastage of only ten per cent.

In the field of promotional literature, as in everything else, the makers of Mother Seigel's Curative Syrup had their own idiosyncratic approach. Their *Almanac* for 1890 took as its theme the dread of old age; this was hardly a positive and optimistic theme with which to associate their products. But there was logic behind the choice. "We all dread to grow old, but the powers of Mother Seigel's Curative Syrup can keep us well and hearty years after we should otherwise be as useless as old hulks of ships forgotten and abandoned on some lonely coast." But Mother Seigel had not finished with her hapless patrons. The *Almanac* has a page for each month on which appears the calendar for that month, and a series of homilies or thoughts for the day; the whole is illustrated by the portraits of some famous personality. There are two for each one, "as they now appear, and as they will appear when old". Sarah Bernhardt, Gustave Eiffel, and Thomas Edison were among the twelve celebrities to suffer this indignity, inflicted with all the ugliness of the nineteenth-century engraver at his worst. If this kind of campaign could sell a product then the Victorian's faith in the power of advertising can be understood. Other promotional items were less depressing than the *Almanac*. It is almost a relief to turn to Holloway's *Almanac and Family Friend* for 1898, which is devoted to blood sports, for example, kangaroo hunting, moose hunting, fox hunting and bull fighting.

It is easy, in the age of the motor car, to forget the impact made by the railways in the nineteenth century. Then, as now, it was a simple matter for all but the poorest to visit London for a day's shopping from the home counties. The speed of rail transport was often not much slower a hundred years ago than it is today; indeed journey times made by crack Victorian express trains are only being bettered in our own generation. Towns and villages that the railway passed by might remain havens of rural peace for a few more decades, but others were part of a countrywide network of rapid communications. Inevitably local traders felt the effect. Some of their most profitable trade was threatened as local wealthy families took to buying in bulk from London wholesalers, or went up themselves to enjoy a day's shopping in the capital.

The small provincial business fought back. One result was *The Family Goldmine*, a kind of house journal issued by an embryonic trade association. It was printed and published for the Proprietors of the Bright Thoughts Publishing Company by Judd and Company Ltd, of Doctors Commons, London, E.C. Ironically, even as they tried self-help, the anxious provincial merchants were fattening up yet another London business. *The Family Goldmine* seems to have been circulated throughout the home counties, and even further afield, so the costs of production could be amortized on a large print run. Of course, if it was too obviously a mass circulation London-based product it would defeat its own purpose. The introduction was a lengthy encomium on the advantages of relying on local traders, with dire warnings of what to expect from the unscrupulous merchants of the capital; this was common to all the editions. But the magazine was printed with a variety of titles and cover designs, and some inside pages were devoted to matters of local interest.

Described as "a compendium of useful household and general knowledge", the magazine consisted of fifty-two pages, 12 by 9 inches, and was in two main sections. The first consisted of twelve double page spreads, each devoted to one type of product – shoes, tea, surgical appliances or whatever. The left hand page carried a short article of about 750 words packed with historical tit-bits about the products. Each essay ended with a paragraph driving home the message of the introduction, and was faced by a blank page given over to the handbills or rubber-stamped ads of local merchants. The second section, which occupied the remaining twenty-eight pages, contained chapters of recipes, gardening hints, cures for children's complaints, a family doctor section, miscellaneous information, and even "Gems from Literature". Many similar promotions were put out by other provincial chambers of commerce, although few were as elaborate. *My Tradesmen: a guide to making purchases for visitors to Oxford* was a more modest enterprise. Brought out in 1882 it was a four page circular, albeit handsomely printed in gilded inks, representing some of Oxford's principal tradesmen.

Yet the provincial merchant was usually outdone by his London rival. In 1867, A. Lynes and Son, Merchant Taylors and Boys' Outfitters of Shoreditch and Kensington, launched an illustrated magazine of fiction and fashion. It appeared twice a year under such catchy titles as *Romance and Reality* or *Novelettes and Novelties*. It was filled with short stories, poems and essays edited by Arthur Lynes himself, and given free to his customers. Volume XII, *Romance and Reality*, carried seven sizeable contributions ranging from *A Big Day With Fate* by J. Linnaeus Banks to *My Only Child* by Mr Lynes. Indeed, this shopkeeper-publisher claimed a small place in the literary world of his times. His journal for promoting gent's suiting enabled him to publish many a literary gem – *A Set of Quadrilles*, *Fairest of the Fair* and *One of These Days* to name a few.

Another editor, risking the rigours of the copyright law, pirated one of the stories and was immediately taken to court. Accordingly, Lynes warned his readers in 1873 that: "Country editors, dramatists and others are reminded that the entire contents of this magazine are the exclusive property of A. Lynes and Son. In the High Court of Chancery, Lord Justice James has granted a perpetual injunction restraining the *Man of Ross* newspaper from pirating Mr A. Lynes story *Girls Together*."

Each number was introduced by a paean of self-congratulation, both on the elegant level of the literary contributions, and on the flourishing state of trade, all made possible by the generous patronage of the customers. The editor drew attention to the layout of his magazine which kept editorial copy and advertisements in two unrelated sections, and so spared the reader the irritation of turning up an advertisement when he was absorbed in the plot of *Angeline in Distress*. Not all shopkeepers took the same view of the place of advertising. In 1887, Charles Baker published a *London Street Guide* with several entries in the section "Places of Interest" that mentioned one of the group's shops and the bargains to be had there.

But Baker's *A.B.C. Guide to London* provided a real service. It comprised fifteen pages of detailed street maps of the metropolis from Holloway in the north down to Battersea in the south, and from Notting Hill Gate east to Poplar. A comprehensive index was included, much valuable information on places of interest to the tourist, and a welter of statistics drawn from the 1881 census. The whole was backed up with twenty-four pages of advertising in the form of an illustrated catalogue of Messrs Baker's men's and boys' clothing. Speaking of the statistics, did the readers of Baker know that, of 127 people killed in street accidents in 1881, 20 were mown down by cabs? Whether any of London's four Serbians were among their number the *A.B.C.* omits to mention.

Promotions and give-aways of all kinds were immensely popular with the Victorian consumer and advertisers often responded on a truly lavish scale. To launch the production of the melodrama *The Dead Heart*, produced at the Adelphi in November 1859, no fewer than 5 million handbills were distributed. They were supplemented with a variety of gimmick give-aways, including 1 million cards in the shape of a heart; 30,000 small cut-outs of "the guillotine scene" and 2,000 "six sheet cuts of the Bastille". Naturally enough advertisers were heartily encouraged in this kind of spending by the agents and one of the most ambitious promotions was offered in the trade press by the Central London Agency to any advertiser who could afford the price. It was no less than the opportunity to enter the field of book publishing. The agency was offering sets of the "Hundred Best Books" at 25 shillings the set to be given away in return for the labels or wrappers of the advertiser's product. "A few weeks back," ran the Central Agency's selling copy, "the whole of the English press was ringing with the offers by various publishers of One Hundred Books at prices ranging from £7 the set upwards and they were extolled by newspapers all over the country as the acme of excellence and cheapness." Obviously, the advertiser who could give away such works with his product had a very strong selling point.

5
EDITORS, ADVERTISERS AND AGENTS

By the end of Victoria's reign, advertising was firmly launched in England. The English had still much to learn from America, as agents and the Americans themselves never tired of repeating. Even so most of the promotion techniques so proudly proclaimed across the Atlantic "herring pond" were known and practised in England. Proof of the advanced state of the art was given by the Niagara Hall Exhibition of Advertising held in London from 22 April to 6 May 1899, and organized by the firm of S. H. Benson. Even then, Bensons were one of London's largest agencies – a staff photograph taken to commemorate the event shows 65 men, 2 women and 11 boys – and the show was on a big scale. It was not the first exhibition of its kind in Europe (there had been a smaller and less successful display at Amsterdam in 1897), but it was the first one of real importance. Most of the 150 exhibitors were British; but Holland was also well represented and stands were entered by French and German exhibitors.

The purpose of the exhibition was, of course, to push home the simple message, it pays to advertise. Here the businessman found promotional ideas he could buy, artists he could hire, and agents willing to handle everything for him. But, if he wanted to do his own advertising, plenty of free advice was offered. One agent had set up a complete programme for a three month publicity campaign treated in four ways: by newspaper and periodical, by bill posting, by house to house distribution, and by point of sale promotion. If he was willing to hear the sales talk the visitor could have the whole thing costed out, and hear a lot of valuable additional information – all for nothing. At another stand he could obtain a comparative costing for various types of campaign in different parts of the country, and make a leisurely survey of the provincial papers. If he had a cutting of one of his own ads with him he could have the typography and layout improved on the spot by a professional.

Every one clearly enjoyed themselves. The organizers were certainly content. For weeks before the opening all the stands had been taken. More or less everything had been provided for the potential client and there was plenty to divert the casual visitor. A special attraction was the display by the Electric Sign Company which had rigged up a unit that spelled out brand names letter by letter. In the early days of electricity this was a great novelty and from morning to evening an eager crowd was to be seen playing the "guess-the-name" game. Another excitement was the phonograph on the *News of the World* stand. There was nothing particularly original about the recorded message; the general gist was "Buy the *News of the World*" with music and commentary added to spin it out. But for nearly all the visitors the talking machine was still something very novel, and the idea that anyone would set one up simply to attract attention, inevitably attracted attention.

The first sight that greeted the visitor in the entrance hall was a tram car with ads. These were devised by J. W. Courtenay who had the sole agency for public transport advertising in most large towns. The tram was flanked by a van from the Carriers' Van Company, and a coach promoting *Famora* toilet soap. This kind of mobile advertisement hoarding had a long history and was still often seen around 1900. One Belfast company had a miniature stage coach specially built to carry advertisements and had it drawn daily through the streets of the city by a team of thoroughbred Shetland ponies. Similarly, a London manufacturer built advertisement hand carts that "could be easily drawn by a boy."

The exhibition entrance hall was surrounded by the stalls of agents and smaller exhibitors; the stands in the main hall were shared between the printers, the large agents, and the large advertisers. Many of the big companies like Pears were quite happy to show off their promotional material as a guide to their smaller brethren, and as a chance for further promotion. A special feature of this section were the specimen window displays. Window dressing was already an important commercial art, in England as well as America. The Erasmic Soap Company spent a small fortune to engage Mr Sidney Priday a leading American practitioner and send him on a promotional tour of Australia and New Zealand.

While some printers displayed their presses and other advanced equipment, most concentrated on displaying their "novelties", trade cards and posters. Raphael Tuck had an impressive display of these novelties – manufactured speculatively, ready for printing with the name of the company that bought them. Among the Dutch printers in this section were the companies of J. H. de Bussy and Senefelder, the latter exhibiting a number of posters designed by Van Caspel who worked exclusively for this firm. One poster which showed the figure of a woman "very boldly treated" and holding aloft a light, was thought to be an especially good buy for a lighting company. Among the better designs of the English companies were those of Louis Rhead done for the Leeds firm of Julian Green. Upstairs in the gallery, many other specimen posters were on offer, not by the printers but by the artists themselves. These had been chosen by a group of leading poster artists, among them Dudley Hardy, Phil May and John Hassall. The designs ranged from black and white and coloured posters to newspaper advertisements, and all were for sale. Since they had been produced speculatively they did not specify any products. Number 15 by John Hassall, it was said, would lend itself to any food or drink product. A design for a bicycle manufacturer might have to be more specific, but even here the poster might be used for an alternative message.

The Exhibition was a great social success. It had been supported by all the main advertisers and agents, the attendance figures ran into the thousands; the Duke of York had asked for a copy of a poster advertising Robb's Biscuits. Each day another crowd of satisfied customers thronged to the exits delighted by the novel attractions. A special hit was the music of the Bolero Ladies' Orchestra, conducted to loud applause by Miss Florence Meiter. Many visitors regretted that the fair musicians rejected the shouts for encores, but this was a small blemish on a highly diverting entertainment. Yet beneath all the gaiety there were stormy undercurrents. The press moguls had been invited to the exhibition, but the relations between newspapers and advertising men were tense. Trouble began at the press lunch held to open the exhibition on 21 April. After an enjoyable banquet came the speeches, among them one by Mr Walter of *The Times*. Things grew more interesting when Sir George Newnes rose to his feet. He had a few jokes to tell, such as how Mr Barratt, the famous advertising manager of Pears, talked his way into the Members' club of the House of Commons even before he became an M.P. The assembled agents were delighted. But they were not to enjoy this fun for long. The struggle between the newspaper proprietor, determined to be absolute ruler of his own pages, and the advertiser fighting for maximum space and freedom of presentation, was of long standing. As far as Newnes was concerned the fight was still on. Continuing in his bantering vein Sir George reminded the advertisers of their place in the scheme of things. Advertisers, he joked, should never forget how much they owed to the publishers; without the press the whole structure of modern advertising would collapse; huge fortunes had been made almost entirely thanks to the columns of the press. Even in the smoke-filled brandy haze, this could not be allowed to go unanswered.

The advertising men awaited the reply of S. H. Benson, the organizer of the affair, and for the moment their champion. He did not fail them. Without for a moment departing from the urbane tone set by Sir George Newnes, he declared that the newspaper man's was misleading. Indeed, said Benson, without the advertisers the press would be in a sorry plight (how right future events proved him to be). Advertisement revenue was the bread and butter of newspaper economics and, if Sir George thought that was too strong, he would surely not deny that at least it provided the butter. Nothing had been said that a gentleman could take offence at, but for a moment a state of conflict was revealed. Within a few months it was to flare up into a full scale campaign, waged by the advertisers against the inflated circulation claims of the proprietors.

However, during the exhibition there were no more of these auguries of war; and things drew to a happy conclusion in the Smoking Concert held on the last evening. Here the Bolero Ladies Orchestra featured as prominently as ever. The gem of the whole evening was unquestionably Miss Beatrice Pettitt's rendering of *Queen of the Earth* as a cornet solo; but then, to cries of astonished delight, came *When the Lights are Low* as an encore! The ladies had relented at last; nothing was wanting to make the final celebrations of the Advertising Exhibition of 1899 an unqualified success.

The first shot in the campaign to force reliable circulation figures out of the newspapers was fired in the new *Advertisers' Review* of 8 April 1899. With a nice sense of timing the journal had been launched just a fortnight before the Niagara Hall Exhibition opened, a fact which prompted accusations that it was sponsored by some anonymous agent. Mathers, F. C. Charles and

Smith's Mutual Advertising Agency were among those cast as the *eminence grise*, but the favourite candidate was of course S. H. Benson himself, whose Exhibition the *Review* so enthusiastically heralded. These persistent rumours led him to issue an official denial in the form of a letter, published in the issue for 1 May. The editors, too, keen to silence the scandalmongers, claiming that, unlike most other advertising publications, they were entirely independent. Whatever the case, their stand on the issue of newspaper circulations should have met with enthusiastic backing from advertisers and agents alike.

The first article – "Guaranteed Circulations: Are they frequently a myth?" – was written more in sorrow than in anger. It began by reviewing recent articles in the London *Figaro* contraverting the claims of "a large London publishing house". (Later the *Review* named the offender as Harmsworth Publications.) Drawing attention to practices not entirely unknown to later generations, the *Review* claimed that publishers sometimes quoted figures that were out of date, or referred to the peak circulations of special issues or selected periods. "It is quite possible," he went on, "that if a really thorough and searching investigation as to the circulation could be obtained, the advertising value of many publications now in good repute would be heavily reduced. . . . The advertiser, confronted by the ever growing number of publications may well wonder if he is not the person who has to find the profit."

This was mild stuff compared with what was to follow, but for the moment the editors were keeping calm. The next step was a "letter to the editor" from someone signing himself Guarantor. He agreed heartily with everything that the *Review* had to say on the subject and proposed that a committee be formed of advertisers, proprietors and agents to scrutinize the books of any newspaper willing to co-operate, and to certify the circulation figures. The editors must have thought well of "Guarantor" 's idea, for the same issue contained a reply coupon for those prepared to attend a meeting. This meeting did not take place for several months partly, it seems, because of the obstruction from the big agencies. They objected to a committee in which the smaller firms would have an equal voice with them, and in any case they could see no cause for action; they had, or were developing, systems to protect their own clients. The *status quo* suited the big agencies well enough. With their resources and influence they could easily protect their clients, or conceal inconvenient facts. Either way they increased their prestige and *clientèle*.

The *Advertisers' Review* conceded that, in the words of one of the largest advertisers of the day, some agents were "the biggest set of thieves in the country". But this did not lessen the *Review*'s fury against those publications which had for years been "fattening on the proceeds of fraudulent trickery and extortion of which the advertiser has had to bear the brunt". Quite apart from false circulation claims, the advertiser had other malpractices to contend with. For example, the dummy copies hawked around by new periodicals to drum up advertisements were "infinitely superior" in printing, quality of paper and design to the finished product. The advertisements were often printed on lower grade paper than that used for the editorial copy and, final indignity, magazines were occasionally printed in two batches. One was of high quality, run off in small quantities to show the advertisers. The second batch, of the lowest possible quality, was distributed to the subscribers.

Yet it was the misrepresentation of circulation figures that really angered the advertisers. It could be quite unashamed. The advertisement manager of one well-known illustrated weekly, whose real circulation was around 12,000, quoted 40,000 in his sales pitch to a London West End shop. But he had been forestalled. The shopkeeper informed him that he had just been talking to a rival publisher who claimed 65,000 (the real figure was nearer 14,000). The first man, somewhat abashed, remarked that this might be an exaggeration. "My dear Sir," said the shopkeeper with delicate irony, "I know it for a fact, the publisher told me so himself."

If publishers regularly lied about their circulation figures, it is hardly surprising that their "canvassers" quoted any figure that came into their head so long as it produced an order. The system had rested on fraud so long that it seemed a pity to disturb it. True, only ten years earlier Louis Collins had proved that agencies, including some of the biggest, were willing to use the system for their own ends; but a scandal is quickly forgotten. What really put the fat in the fire was the discovery by T. B. Browne, a leading agent, that his own firm had been fooled by a couple of twopenny-halfpenny reps. On Tuesday, 11 April 1899, William Fitzroy Berkeley and Joseph William Norfolk were brought up at the Old Bailey before the common sergeant, Sir Forest Fulton, to be sentenced for conspiring to defraud Messrs T. B. Browne Ltd by means of false circulation certificates. They escaped lightly with three months between them. They might have felt themselves unlucky – they were only caught because their employers, the Morgan Publishing Company, went into liquidation. With all the Company books in the hands of the Receiver, it was impossible to conceal these malpractices from the public.

The Morgan case seems to have had a cathartic effect on the British advertising community. Urged on by the *Advertisers' Review* clients began to make a stand on their rights, demanding proof of circulations, and refusing payment until it was forthcoming. When asked for proof one publisher produced a printer's certificate, but even this did not satisfy the client who suspected that the printer had a financial interest in the publication. Accordingly he demanded an independent scrutiny of the books and the matter quietly lapsed. In another case the advertiser simply refused to pay until presented with a more realistic bill. A good deal of huffing and puffing ensued, at the end of which, rather than take his customer to court the publisher abruptly agreed to settle for £8 in lieu of the original demand for £60.

The debate over circulations was being followed with some interest in America. *Printers' Ink,* which had taken a brotherly interest in the *Advertisers' Review* from its first number, seems to have felt that the English were being over-critical. In their view the number of copies circulated so closely matched the number printed that the two were virtually identical. It dismissed, as altogether too expensive and troublesome, the notion that a publisher might overprint merely to inflate his circulation figures. Such things did happen, but most of the papers in question were not worth taking seriously. Nor did *Printers' Ink* accept that a printer with a vested interest in a publication might be prepared to exaggerate the print run. But it did concede that the conscientious proprietor might discover the net circulation figures if he troubled to count all returned copies and deduct them from the print run. *Printers' Ink* felt that papers like the Washington *Star* or the St Louis *Republic* that did this, were seeking a perfection that "the advertiser who knows his business does not regard as material or important, and are at the same time putting their figures at a disadvantage when they are compared with others". Most advertisers were content to know that papers like the New York *World* and *Journal,* which did not even quote their print runs, were putting out inflated circulation figures, and steered clear of them.

Yet for all their Yankee cunning the editors of *Printers' Ink* had still missed a trick. Suppose even the quantity sold – let alone the quantity printed – was actually *higher* than the quantity read? In England some publications had vast sales which allowed them to raise advertisement rates even though their readership figures were well below their sales. The secret lay in the craze for competitions that had swept the country. The villain of the piece, from the advertisers' point of view at least, was Harmsworth Publications. To promote his penny weeklies *Answers* and *Home Chat* Alfred Harmsworth ran a competition for 1,000 guineas to go to the entrant who most nearly guessed the number of births recorded in one week in Britain's major cities. Any number of entries could be made, so long as each was accompanied by the entry coupon printed in the magazine. Readers were urged to shorten the odds in their favour by buying up as many copies as they could lay their hands on. The English public, with its "sporting proclivities", responded with gusto. Some entrants apparently bought several thousand copies apiece. *Advertisers' Review* quotes figures for another competition run by the *Home Companion*. This was not one of Harmsworth's journals, but it saw the lottery as an excellent way of promoting sales. Even though the only prize was a £20 bicycle, still the magic worked. The bicycle was to go to the reader who sent in "*the greatest number of these forms*" – the italics are theirs – and "If any reader sends 1,000 forms or over, and does not get this bicycle because some one has sent a few more, we shall present that reader with a certificate for £8, entitling him to get this £20 bicycle for £12." Who could resist? Even though 1,000 copies of a penny magazine would cost you £8 10s (a happy chance for the publisher) you were still £7 10s to the good if you were aiming to get a new bicycle and, with luck, you might get it for less. The populace did their sums and bought their copies – in the case of the winner of the previous competition no fewer than 1,705!

The *Advertisers' Review* looked with a jaundiced eye at all such practices. "If people will send in 1,705 forms to win a £20 bicycle, how many will they send in to win 1,000 guineas?" The answer was all too clear and no good could come of it for the advertisers:

> "You have a very poor circulation," observed the doctor.
> "Sir," replied the indignant publisher, "my circulation is sworn to at 200,000 copies."

Swapping such tired chestnuts with its readers the *Advertisers' Review* kept up the fight, but in its heart of hearts it saw victory only in the remote future.

Meanwhile other battles had to be fought. We next find these indefatigable journalists switching their attack from the publishers to some of the largest of London's agencies. The object of their anger was the old practice of "farming".

In the early days of advertising "farming" had been straightforward enough. The agent contracted with a newspaper to buy space in bulk over a long period, and for this he earned a discount on the standard rate. The publisher was happy to sell in bulk; and the agent could offer his client cut rates, or supplement his commission by reselling at the standard rate. Henry Sell had described the procedure in his *Press Directory* in the 1860s; it was common practice and he saw no reason to apologise for it. In his view the links between newspaper, agent, and advertiser were like those between manufacturer, wholesaler, and retailer. Other agents advanced other arguments in support of the practice. Because bulk buying guaranteed them an assured revenue, the newspapers respected the large agent who could therefore act with more independence than his smaller colleagues. Unlike them he could afford to ignore "the down-at-heel proprietors of useless publications, whom many of the smaller fry of agents are tempted to approach on an understanding of mutual benefit to the detriment of those whose interests they cannot afford to study, even if they are honest enough to do so". The "stuffy" Victorians certainly had a refreshingly open manner when discussing their business rivals. But the laws of libel had to be observed; and the *Advertisers' Review*, which had its enemies, trod carefully through the minefield it was trying to clear. The abuses of the system were basically three. First the "help-one-another-agents": committed to buying sizable areas of space, the agent did not always find it easy to fill them, so naturally enough a freemasonry of mutual aid evolved. While planning a client's campaign the agent would recommend media farmed by his collaborator, secure in the knowledge that he would do the same for him. The two media might well appeal to the same market and so be alternatives rather than complementary but this hardly mattered so long as the client – relying on his agent – believed that the campaign was being given a wide spread. Secondly, even if he was not the victim of an arrangement like this, the client was urged to advertise in the media farmed by the agent, irrespective of their suitability. Thirdly, the impression of cheap advertising which the farming agents could give by their cut rates, was an illusion: these cheap rates were simply loss leaders. The agent who held the sole franchise for a publication was in an enviable position. The small agent had to deal through him if one of his clients wanted space in such a publication. But the farming agent could always offer the same space at a cheaper price. And this he often did, writing direct to the client, and pointing out how much he could save by dealing direct – and implying that he would enjoy the same terms in all their dealings. In reality the large agency recouped on such discounts by over-charging for other services. The small man could do little if a powerful rival decided to pirate his *clientèle* like this. His best defence was to find a journal that would give him sole rights over its advertising. So the system spread.

The *Advertisers' Review* launched the attack bravely, naming two of London's largest agencies as offenders; but it was obliged to pull its punches to avoid legal action. Even in naming Messrs T. B. Browne and Smith's Agency, the *Review* was careful to dub the one "a firm of agents of the very highest standing, whose name is synonymous with honest and straightforward business transactions" and to describe the manager of the other as "a gentleman of strict Christian principles". The following week it published a letter from a reader upholding the system of farming; he thought that the *Review* had weakened its case by singling out two firms which, by its own confession, were above reproach. The editor did not evade the issue. "We are in rather an unfortunate position," he wrote. "If we mention names in connection with this practice we are compelled to qualify our statements with an assurance of the honest intentions of the firms we name, however much we might like to make the statement without the qualification, or else we should render ourselves liable for libel action."

Leaving the lawyers to sort out the implications of those remarks, the article went on to examine the charges. The real case was that T. B. Browne farmed the advertisements for Harmsworth's *Answers* but not those for the similar *Tit-Bits* and *Pearsons Weekly*; however, at least half the advertisement space in *Answers* was sold to Browne's clients but not a single one of these appeared in the other two papers. Still more interesting, thought the *Review*, was the fact that many of Smith's clients also appeared in *Answers* while many of Browne's advertisers were found to have taken space in *Great Thoughts* published by Smith's Advertising Agency.

The reliability of a farming agent's advice was, to say the least, open to question. Nor was it sufficient to argue that the clients, all hard-headed businessmen, should look after themselves. In many cases they simply could not, since a farming agent rarely disclosed any of his own newspaper interests, and never revealed that he had interests in other media that he proposed, through his connections with the agents that likewise farmed them. In any case, since the client paid his agent for advice about the media, there was little point in always questioning that advice. But incensed by the revelations in the

C.1 *Bubbles* by Sir John Millais F.R.A., for many years the best known work of art throughout the British Empire—thanks to Thomas J. Barratt of Pears

C.2 These pictures show another popular advertiser's promotion. Many manufacturers offered these little cardboard models as children's toys. Bovril had the good sense to see that their name was prominent on the front; a military operation planned over a cup of Bovril could hardly fail. Prices, the soap manufacturers responsible for the charming little boat, would perhaps have been forgotten less quickly had they given it the name of their product!

C.3 Besides giving away this harmless gimmick, the Carbolic Smoke Ball Co. also unwisely offered £100 to anyone not cured by their product. In 1892 a Mrs Carlill, who actually *caught* flu after using the smoke ball, took the astonished company to law and was awarded her £100

CARBOLIC SMOKE BALL
GIVES INSTANT RELIEF

C.4 Cycling, the vogue of the 1880's and 1890's, was featured in many advertisements

C.5 The proprietor of Eno's Fruit Salt was too serious to be interested in sport. When he was not propounding somewhat obscure metaphysics he used space for prestige advertising

C.6 In an age when milk was often diluted with water and chalk the claim "Guaranteed Absolutely Pure", if it could be maintained, certainly had sales potential

C.7 In Hood's Sarsaparilla the health beverage market found a strong competitor from across the Atlantic. In those days adapting the product to the market seems to have gone to the length of specially calculated calendars

C.8 "Every picture tells a story", the maxim of much academic art of the time, inevitably appealed to the advertisers. An elegant variation of this style is found in this Rowntree's cocoa advertisement

Review one advertiser took his agent to task and demanded to see the books and records of the media that he farmed. After trying to fob him off the agent bluntly refused, and the client departed – "boiling over with indignation and suspicion as to his method of doing business".

As the campaign rumbled on, there emerged quite a flourishing trade among farming agents big and small selling their clients' ads in return for future considerations. The relative merits of the media had little if anything to do with the case. The big agency with space to spare on a large appropriation naturally looked around for someone to barter it with. The *Review*'s reforming drive included a list of agents who did not farm, and the editors offered this free promotion to any agent who cared to ask for it. The fact that they never recruited more than twenty names suggests that however "iniquitous" the practice, most agents were content with it.

The conflict of interest between an editor and his advertisers aroused lively controversy even in the offices of the *Illustrated London News* although this journal is probably the first major news medium to have taken full page display advertising. At the first shareholders' meeting of a new company formed to carry on the *News* and the *Sketch*, held in June 1899, at least one shareholder had a complaint to make. A regular subscriber since the first number in 1842, Leighton had once had a complete set of the paper, but had been forced to part with it for lack of space. How much better if the advertisements could be confined to separate pages as they were in some other papers. "The great thing is to keep the advertisements in their proper place and to have a good newspaper and an historical record that was worth keeping."

Leighton was applauded by the meeting, but the chairman Sir William Ingram declared – "We have our views upon the subject, but unfortunately for us the advertisers have theirs." In fact the advertisers had strong views. If ads were put on pages which could be easily torn out in the interests of an "Historical record", what, they wanted to know, was the point of advertising? "We want our advertisements to go into your newspaper so that they can reside there comfortably and as obtrusively as possible." Showing a firmer grip on publishing realities than Sir George Newnes in his speech at the Niagara Hall Exhibition, Ingram added – "We live by advertisements. Without advertisements this paper could not be carried on except at enormous loss."

If this was true of the *Illustrated London News* it was certainly true of the rest of the press. In 1902 it was estimated that the *Daily Telegraph*'s annual advertising revenue amounted to some £200,000, while that of *The Times* fifteen years earlier was thought almost to double that figure. The case of *The Times* is especially interesting. Its huge prestige and large circulation – far greater than any other daily in the first half of Victoria's reign – combined to produce this large advertising revenue, which in turn enabled it to improve its services still further. The operation at Printing House Square, London, was a marvel to contemporaries. The "Walter machines" that printed 22,000 to 24,000 sheets per hour were revolutionary when first introduced; the newspaper seized on every technical innovation that could be pressed into service.

In August 1877, barely a year after Alexander Bell first patented his telephone, there were 780 telephones in Great Britain. Eight years later the figure soared to 325,500. The advertising agents were among the most enthusiastic advocates of the new instrument, and Thomas Smith of the Mutual Advertising Agency featured his telephone as a special attraction to his clients, especially the American ones. Smith offered another service to American customers, a service of which the telephone was an integral feature. Not only did he send copies of English newspapers for inspection and accept letters for firms without a London address, both fairly commonplace services, but he let his offices for short periods to people choosing their own premises in London. On arrival in England, Americans found themselves in immediate contact with more than 6,000 of London's leading firms through the telephone of the Mutual Advertising Agency.

Newspaper offices quickly made use of this new development in communications. A special line connected the editorial offices of *The Times* with the Houses of Parliament so that debates could be reported almost at once. During the Congress of Berlin (1878) *The Times* expended £800 on telegrams alone, and so could publish the text of the treaty almost upon its signature. Such figures staggered contemporaries, but they generally recognized that it was advertising revenue which made them possible. Indeed, *Lloyds Weekly Newspaper*, with a circulation of more than 100,000, claimed that it was refusing pages of advertising every week, and thinking of putting up its rates.

In view of the known value of advertising to newspaper revenues, one wonders how the editors held the advertisers at bay for so long. In both England and America they manfully fought off demands for the freedom of the page until, in 1875, the *Illustrated London News* conceded an entire page to Pulvermacher's Galvanic Chain Bands and Belts. Before this, advertisers had resorted to every typographical atrocity to sidestep the editor's ban on large type sizes, or to do away with the column rules to make way for large displays. One trick was to take up several column inches with an endless repetition of the maker's name and product. Another was to build up large capital letters by grouping together smaller capitals. An example of this ruse was the spreading of the name "Cuticura" across the eight columns. All the proprieties were observed – the column rules were retained, and large type sizes were avoided. The result may have been appalling to contemplate but the editor's sense of decorum overrode their feeling for typographical decencies and the feeling of their compositors. The ban on large illustrations was just as rigid. In the early 1860s the impresario of the opera *Robin Hood* took a full page, and forbidden to use any form of display he used the space to print the libretto in full. It was imaginative, useful and possibly surprising, but unquestionably it lacked the impact of a dramatic scene from the action.

After 1875, however, the revolution in the appearance of the newspaper pages was rapid. Within ten years of the historic decision of the *Illustrated London News*, Thomas Smith, writing in his house publication *Successful Advertising*, had this to say: "Anyone who has followed the developments in advertising will be struck by the immense increase in the number of illustrated advertisements. Not very long ago whole page advertisements consisted nine tenths of type matter only. Now it is the other way."

6
POSTERS AND PAINTERS: THE BIRTH OF A NEW ART

In the late Victorian age a new "horror" raised its head. Soon came a "plague of flashing electric light advertisements and sky signs in our cities". The phrase was used in a letter to *The Times*. One of the letter's fifteen signatories was the artist and designer Walter Crane who had produced his first poster some forty years previously. In those days the "excesses" of the poster artists and bill stickers had raised a similar outcry from the diehards. But advertisers had always claimed – if they thought about the matter at all – that the hoardings, far from being an eyesore, were a kind of poor man's art gallery and so rendered a public service. Crane himself had been one of the first to make this claim really mean something in England.

In Paris the poster had long been a serious art form. In the 1890s the open air exhibition provided by Parisian advertisement hoardings was compared with the "museum" of marble and bronze in the streets of Florence. It was in France that the coloured lithographic poster had been born, and from the outset it had been treated seriously. By the 1880s pioneers led by Ernest Maindron had made the study of posters a branch of connoisseurship and in

1889 Maindron organized the first exhibition devoted to the poster. Held in Paris it illustrated the history of poster techniques from the seventeenth century. The exhibition launched a new vogue, with other towns quickly following suit, and the next year the Grolier Club held an exhibition of French posters in New York. True to their enthusiasm for everything new, the Americans became keen devotees and, as Jane Abdy writes in her excellent book *The French Poster*, by 1896 there were estimated to be 6,000 collectors in the States alone. London's first poster exhibition was held in 1894 and the English had only had time to realize that the advertising hoarding could be attractive before they discovered that it was potentially valuable too.

The sponsor of the exhibition, held at the Aquarium exhibition hall, was the printer and dealer, Edward Bella who, single handed, created the English collector's market in posters. The exhibition contributed greatly to this and the foreword to the catalogue, written by J. Thacher Clarke, one of Bella's friends and himself a collector, was calculated to get the well-to-do reaching into their pockets to be in at the start of a cheap but authentic artistic vogue.

Clarke begins by pointing to the vivid contemporaneity of the poster – "in no other branch of design do the most characteristic features of every-day life find clearer expression than in the art of the pictorial and mural advertisement". For this reason it would be of major value to the future historian, but primarily it had undoubted artistic merit, having now become a legitimate field for the collector. There is more in the same vein and in a stirring peroration Clarke hails the advance of the poster into territory previously artistically barren as an aesthetic conquest – "Thus does modern art address itself like the epic of old to the crowded market place." Many of the exhibits were from Mr Clarke's own collection, where they were not from the stock of the sponsor Edward Bella, and copies were for sale.

In 1895 the publication of a heavily illustrated history by Charles Hiatt added a contribution to the poster idea. His book drew heavily on Maindron's *L'Affiche illustré* (1886) but was largely illustrated with photographs Hiatt had taken at the exhibition of the previous year and it seems obvious that he knew Bella. Certainly exhibition, catalogue and book made a tidy little promotion which propagated the vogue for poster collecting in the 1890s.

The idea of pictorial advertisement has a long history – there are wall paintings at Pompeii with an obviously commercial purpose – but in modern times the story really starts with the window bills of the seventeenth century.

They became increasingly used and there is a delightful French example from 1715 which advertises collapsible pocket umbrellas, weighing only five or six "*onces*", to be had from Mr Marius in the rue des Fossez, St Germain. In 1836 a technique of colour lithography was perfected and the stage was set for the real development of the colour poster. Hiatt traces its origins to the French passion for illustrated novels published, like those in England, in weekly parts. These were generally advertised on placards carrying enlargements of a cover design or one of the illustrations. Soon publishers began to commission specially designed posters, the first of which appeared in the late 1830s.

It was only when Paul Gavarni, an eminent graphic artist in his own right, started poster design in the 1850s that the poster's potential began to be realized, and in the next decade the artist Manet produced a striking poster. Like the majority of posters at the time, it advertised a book – in this case the illustrated edition of Chamfleury's *Les Chats*. Manet saw that the essence of the new form was simplicity and produced a bold and dramatic design which showed a black and white cat vividly silhouetted against a stormy sky and dark industrial landscape.

From the beginning the poster attracted the interest of professional artists but it remained largely the preserve of the book publishers and was simply one interesting new approach to street advertising among many. The man who made pictorial advertising posters the only possible medium of outdoor publicity and one of the sensations of Paris in the dying years of the second Empire, began his career as an ordinary craftsman.

Jules Chéret was one of the army of lithographers who provided the nineteenth-century publisher with fashion plates and the illustrations of the more expensive books; reproducing on the printer's stone the work of other artists. After a few years in London, where he had hoped to make his fortune but instead designed furniture catalogues for Maples, the young man returned to Paris and, with the help of a rich friend, set up a printing firm in 1868. But Chéret was not only a highly skilled lithographer, he also had a considerable artistic imagination and his first poster in 1866 showed that something brilliant and original had emerged from the generally despised world of the advertiser. Strong in his expertise as a craftsman and quite at home in the pressures of a business environment Chéret developed his imaginative gifts within the framework of advertising to produce the first true commercial art.

The size of his output alone would have made him a major figure in the development years of a new art – he designed more than 1,000 posters – but he performed another great service. His posters became the rage of Paris and manufacturers of all kinds competed for the use of his work. The poster was no longer restricted to the field of book advertising but had become a widely-used medium. Chéret's clients included the Hippodrome, La Diaphone Face Powder, Cosmydor soap, the great store *Aux Buttes Chaumont* as well as the Moulin Rouge, the Folies Bergére and many other theatres. His first posters rapidly became collectors' pieces and as the craze grew enthusiasts pursued their collecting by all means, fair or foul; bill-stickers were bribed and posters mysteriously disappeared from hoardings overnight until printers saw the light and increased their print runs to meet the demand.

Chéret's style was quite original. While some of his contemporaries and many of his less gifted successors designed posters that copied the fashionable art of the salons, he produced a new style; disregarding the conventions of perspective or composition as he saw fit and aiming instead to grab the attention of the passer-by and communicate one simple message. Movement and colour were the keynotes. Blazing reds, hard blues, glowing yellows and vivid greens were thrown together apparently haphazardly; in the 'toy' advertisements for *Aux Buttes Chaumont* the figures burst through the lettering and seemed almost to run out into the street to buttonhole the spectator, while in other examples, such as the poster for Saxoleine paraffin oil, the sweep of an arm forces one's attention to the lamp, glowing brilliant and clear. Occasionally the effect of the poster is weakened by badly designed lettering (the Saxoleine advertisement is a case in point) for, sticking to his trade as a lithographer-designer with rigorous logic, Chéret did not design his own typography. In this one vital aspect Chéret left the pioneering work to others, but after him the line of development for the poster was clear. His designs were an artistic triumph, a commercial success and a public amenity. "Paris without its Chérets," wrote a contemporary, "would be a Paris without one of its most prominent characteristics; a Paris, moreover, with its gaiety of aspect materially diminished."

And there was plenty of room for gaiety in what Huysmans described as the "monotonous sullen grey" Paris that Baron Haussman had designed. In a society that worshipped Goncourt's *joie de vivre* as though it were a new religion, Chéret was one of the high priests. His work was admired by the Goncourts and Degas, collected by Seurat and praised by the art critic of *Le Figaro*. "There is far more talent shown in a poster than in many of the most discussed paintings of the salon" he wrote, and four years later Chéret was awarded the Legion d'Honneur for "creating a new branch of art, by applying art to commercial and industrial printing". The establishment, by conferring the highest accolade, was confirming a universal verdict. "How can we ever be sufficiently grateful to Chéret for having won for art the ever open book of the street" was the view of one intellectual, and Parisians revelled in the riot of gaiety and colour that had invaded their town. They christened his delightful model "*la Chérette*" and copied her clothes, while the artists among them avidly copied the style of the master. In 1900 he designed his last poster and turned to the more dignified business of decorating the Hotel de Ville. He outlived the craze for posters but he was not forgotten. In 1927 a rich collector set up the Chéret Museum in Nice – a memento to a Paris that was past.

Many other talented and original artists had contributed to this "poster school of Paris". Edmond Grasset had already made his name as a painter, designer of stained glass and industrial designer and his eclectic style reflects his painterly inclinations while the colours are more subdued than those of Chéret. Such designs as the charming bill for the *Salon des Cent* exhibition of 1894, the advertisement for Marquet's ink, and even the celebrated theatre bill advertising Sarah Bernhardt as Joan of Arc show marked affinities to the style of William Morris and Burne-Jones. The *Librairie Romantique*, one of the most famous posters of its period, illustrated the nineteenth-century romantic style at its most refined. One of the most striking of all the designs for a commercial advertisement came from the hand of A. Willette whose poster for Van Houten's coffee, showing a Dutch girl, almost "Art Deco" in style, against sinuous leaves, was bold, beautiful and effective. Artists like Pierre Bonnard and Louis Anquetin worked successfully in this commercial field, as well as lesser men such as Jean de Paleologue, with an advertisement for Whitworth's Cycles (1894), and T. A. Steinlen, one of the most enthusiastic and brilliant exponents of the art.

During the 1890s a new trend, soon to dominate advertising, emerged. The "girly" ads of this period, for anything from Electricine lamps to patent household disinfectants, showed what the French artist, let loose among the "gay Parisiennes", could really do in the field of promotion. Before the end of the century the resort of Trouville was advertising its charms through those of a delightful little dolly complete with striped one-piece bathing costume.

As we shall see the English poster painters had nothing to learn about the use of curvaceous females from the French, but before we turn to this we must first look at the work of the two greatest poster artists.

In 1895 Henri de Toulouse-Lautrec, although only thirty-one, had just six more short years to live. The son of an aristocrat he had been tragically crippled in youth, and had left the privileged life to study art in Paris. Despising the conventions of salon art or the theorizing of the later impressionists, he applied his immense talent to painting the men and women of the commercial and theatrical world of Paris, and its brothels and bars. His first poster appeared in 1891, with an impact that could only be compared with that of Chéret a generation earlier. By this time the Parisian public was not only familiar with the posters but expected them to be of the highest quality – "Undoubtedly the commercial poster still exists in France, but the most astute advertising agents, looking at the matter solely from a commercial point of view, find that the really artistic work actually pays better cash results." In a situation like this, mere brilliance and originality was not enough to startle the town. In purely technical achievement Toulouse-Lautrec certainly outstripped the opposition – drama of gestures and movement, compositional placing of the flat colour areas and the dynamic flow of the line were all breathtaking – and, more important in this field, all projected a single visual message. But he also conveyed a force of observation and insight into character that placed him firmly among the greatest names in European art.

Toulouse-Lautrec was at his best painting posters for the cabaret artists who were his friends. His studies of Aristide Bruant and the dancer Jane Avril are outstanding, as is the poster for Caudieux showing the actor hurrying off the stage as if towards the spectator; but it was the artist's fascination with the brilliant singer and impersonator Yvette Guilbert that inspired one of his greatest achievements. Charles Hiatt in his book on the poster, compared the intuitive and realistic art of the *chanteuse* with that of the artist, and accounted for the sympathetic understanding between them in these terms.

Embittered by his deformity and by what he considered a lack of recognition Toulouse-Lautrec, always a heavy drinker, ended his life as an alcoholic in a mental sanatorium. There is a sad footnote to his unhappy life in a report of the London Exhibition of Advertising in 1899 where one of his sketches was shown. The critic writes: "This rough sketch by Lautrec is of especial interest as it may be the last we shall see from his brush, as it has recently become necessary to place him in a lunatic asylum." However, despite his dissolute life, Toulouse-Lautrec had always taken a rigidly professional approach to his work; a deeply inspired artist he was also a highly skilled craftsman lithographer as befitted an admirer of the great Chéret.

Toulouse-Lautrec brought an intensity and profundity to the art of the poster that was not to be equalled, but the purely decorative tradition which was Chéret's great legacy was to be given a new and lyrical dimension by Alfons Mucha who, like so many poster artists, became famous almost overnight.

It was a poster for Sarah Bernhardt in her new role as *Gismonda* which made his name. At the time the great actress, with whose name Mucha's art was to be associated, had never met the Czech artist. He was already in his mid-thirties, but was still virtually unknown to the Parisian public. The divine Sarah had simply given instructions for a poster and as her regular designer was out of Paris the commission fell to Mucha as a "second best". When the poster went up in the Christmas of 1894 crowds assembled outside the theatre to admire it; popular acclaim was endorsed by the art world and by the actress herself who thereafter regularly commissioned her posters from Mucha, paying him the remarkably high fee of 1,500 Fr. for each design. When she toured America she had the lobbies of the theatres decorated with his work and his reputation was rapidly established on both sides of the Atlantic. He was to execute many commercial commissions, such as the famous *Papier Job* for *Job* cigarettes, but his designs for Bernhardt, one of the most famous series of posters ever designed, remain his finest achievement and, according to contemporaries, captured the elusive character of the actress more completely than the work of any other artist or photographer.

In 1894, the year of the Aquarium exhibition in London, the work of Mucha was unknown in England but he was soon to enjoy the same reputation with English connoisseurs as he did elsewhere. At this time the achievements of the French school naturally dominated the dealers' catalogues while of the 200-odd exhibits in the exhibition, all but about 20 were by Parisian artists. Yet if the English started late, they had already thrown up a number of fine designers, with some masterpieces to their credit, while in the next century England was to lead Europe for a time.

The first English pictorial poster seems to have been the one designed by Godfrey Durand for the launching of the weekly illustrated journal the *Graphic* in 1869. Shortly after this Walter Crane produced one for a manufacturer of lead pencils but neither were of particular quality, and the history of the English poster is more usually dated from 1871. In this year Fred.

Walker, well known as a painter, and an associate of the Royal Academy, was commissioned to design a theatre bill for a dramatized version of Wilkie Collins' novel, *The Woman in White.* It was in fact Walker's only poster but, like Manet, he saw that the essential point of the new form was dramatic simplicity. The design is in black and white and the picture is almost filled by the white gown of the woman. As she walks away from the spectator into the blackness of the night she is turning back to beckon to some unseen follower, and the whole effect is one of mystery and suspense. Walker took this commercial commission seriously. Perhaps he knew something of what was happening in France, certainly he was to be proved prophetic in England. To someone who asked how he was going to approach the unusual project he replied: "I am bent on doing all I can with my first attempt at what I consider might develop into an important branch of art." When the organizers of the 1894 exhibition came to search for a copy of Walker's famous poster they found that there was not a copy in existence; only the original cartoon survived, for which the owner was asking no less than seventy guineas. That would be a fair sum now for a graphic by a living artist; then it was astronomical and indicates the prestige that Walker's "branch of art" had won even in his own lifetime.

A number of English academic painters were to follow Walker's example though they had less success in the new genre than their opposite numbers in France. Among the best was Sir Anthony Linton's design for a performance of *Anthony and Cleopatra* in 1874, while Edward Poynter's advertisement for the Guardian Assurance Company, showing the Roman goddess Minerva flanked by columns, had, at least, the merit of solidity that insurance companies admire. But none of the English art establishment achieved anything that could be compared with the work of Gavarni and Grasset in France. Sir Herbert Herkomer R.A. earned a certain reputation for somewhat overelaborate and heavy design, but more interesting is the fact that he was teaching at the Bushey College of Art at the time when James Pryde and William Nicholson were studying there. As the Beggarstaff Brothers these two artists were later to produce some of the finest English posters.

During the 1870s nothing was produced in England to equal Fred. Walker's splendid poster. Pear's, who made a sensation by their exploitation of Millais' sentimental painting *Bubbles,* did something for authentic poster design when they commissioned the successful advertisement *Monks Shaving.* But it was in the 1880s that the commercial emphasis, essential in any product advertising, was firmly introduced to the British poster. In 1880 Walter Crane returned to the scene with a poster advertising the Promenade Concerts at Covent Garden. His other designs included the cover of the English *Illustrated Magazine*, enlarged for the advertisement hoardings, and a pretty little piece, following the style of Morris and Burne-Jones, for the Hau champagne company of Reims. But more important was the name of Dudley Hardy. Already successful as an illustrator and painter he made the second essential step beyond simplicity in design of making the typographic element an integral part of the composition.

Hardy started in publisher's advertising with a poster advertising the new magazine *Today*. The "*Today* girl" was a dashing bright-eyed beauty with yellow dress, "saucy" hat and a flying black boa walking out of the poster and daring the viewer to buy the magazine. For the production at the Prince of Wales theatre Hardy painted a *Gaiety Girl*. She was quite a different character. A buxom girl, with plunging neck line and billowing skirts, she cavorted across the scene with all the reckless *joie de vivre* of a figure by Chéret. Outside the theatre itself, thanks to the genius of some forgotten bill sticker, a frieze of the posters made up a line of irresistible chorus girls that made a sensation at the time.

Hardy showed his versatility when he designed the advertisement for another new magazine *St Paul's* launched as a serious literary weekly. Again he used a girl but this time an austere young miss standing decently erect and still – the very symbol of aesthetic appreciation. A study of their sales record was to convince the proprietors that their earnest intentions were not shared by the public and they shortly changed editorial policy. Again Hardy was employed to present a new *St Paul's* image. The poster he designed shows the dome of St Paul's in the distance but in the foreground there is an abandoned "modern" girl seated on the end of a see-saw which pivots on the crescent of the moon; while on the other end sits the Bertie Wooster of the 1880s – ready for anything if someone will kindly tell him what's going on.

Traditionally the poster artist had promoted books, magazines and plays, but Hardy was also a master in the field of product promotion and the poster he designed for Phit-Easi shoes was superb in the way it successfully directed attention to footwear. Hardy was living at a time when there was a distinct fashion of dress for walking, and he utilized this to show a man, girl and child, backs to the spectator so as to reduce interest in them as personalities, walking away into the distance. It was very clear that Phit-Easi shoes were meant for walking.

Maurice Greiffenhagen, another artist who raised the standard of English poster design, produced a remarkable and unique poster for the *Pall Mall Budget* in which he used bold flat areas of colour; but the most renowned of English poster artists was Aubrey Beardsley, who already had a European reputation as an illustrator and designer. He was a leading spirit behind the *Yellow Book* and his advertisement for that journal is a striking example of his style. But the poster he designed for the Avenue Theatre and the first performance of Shaw's *Arms and the Man* was truly revolutionary. Until that time the theatre posters of London, despite the example of Walker's *Woman in White*, were in general undistinguished, the artist being content to highlight some of the action, such as the heroine at death's door or the villain in a moment of devilish triumph. Beardsley, however, depicted the sinister figure of a mysterious woman staring out through two diaphanous curtains. The contrast of solid colour and delicate decorative effects increased the effectiveness of the poster.

The posters produced by Hardy, Greiffenhagen and Beardsley could command prices comparable with the best French work in Paris sale rooms. Hardy's Yellow Girl for *Today* fetched twenty francs while Beardsley's work was still more expensive. It is remarkable that although Beardsley was working at a time when collecting posters was fashionable in London, neither Bella in London nor Sagot in Paris listed his famous *Avenue* poster in their catalogues. It could be assumed from this that within a matter of months the originals had been lost or destroyed – unless, of course, they were snapped up by people connected with the theatre. Beardsley's importance as an artist far exceeds his work in advertising and his fantastic and highly imaginative style found numerous imitators.

Among the best successors of Beardsley in theatre advertising was Albert Morrow. One aspect of his versatile work is seen in the poster he did for the production of *The New Woman*, a strong and geometric design utterly different from the poster using a bouncy and scantily-dressed girl he did to advertise the magazine *Illustrated Bits*.

Among the younger artists who appeared in the nineties the Beggarstaff Bradley settled in Chicago where, from the mid-1890s, he produced a series of theatre posters for Irving's production of Beckett indicated the arrival of a new style, bold, simple and effective. The Beggarstaff's hallmark was their evocative placing of flat areas of colour – often blacks or dark tones on dull-coloured paper – and nowhere was it more effective than in their posters for the special issue of *Harper's Magazine*. In these, however, the simple outline of a "Beefeater" is complemented by magnificent lettering. The Beggarstaffs were among the rare band of English artists whose work was eagerly collected in Europe. They later did product advertising and showed four designs at the 1899 Advertising Exhibition, commissioned by "Nobody's" candles and pianos.

American enthusiasm for the French poster did not prevent the rise of a talented native school, though at the outset much of the inspiration and some of the artists were from abroad, notably England. Edward Penfield, born in Brooklyn in 1866, was probably the first artist working in the field, and his designs for *Harper's Bazaar* could challenge comparison with the best of Europe. Perhaps their most striking feature was the superb typography, but in richness and subtlety of colouring they were surpassed by the work of Louis J. Rhead, an Englishman who went to the States in 1883. He had been trained at the South Kensington School of Art and his style, shaped in the tradition of William Morris and Burne-Jones, betrays this English background. But his use of colour in the famous poster for the New York *Sun* broke new ground. It depicts a young woman in the park, drawn in a manner reminiscent of Aubrey Beardsley but having an impact that derives chiefly from the way Rhead uses colour. Clothed in a dress of garnet and red, the woman stands on vivid green grass against a background of golden sky and framed by blue trees. The whole composition is irradiated by a burning crimson sun. In Rhead's poster for "Pearline the Modern Cleanser", the influence of Morris is unmistakable in the way that the girl is drawn, pegging out a dazzling white sheet that hangs square and flat like a placard. He was the first artist working in America to hold an exhibition of his poster designs but occasionally continued to work for English firms, exhibiting on the stand of a Leeds printer at the 1899 Advertisers' Exhibition.

In the work of Will Bradley the style of Aubrey Beardsley took root in America to produce a wild and luxuriant growth. Born in Springfield, Mass., Bradley settled in Chicago where, from the mid-1890s he produced a series of posters and designs for *The Chap Book* in which the wayward brilliance of Beardsley's line was united with a vivid and highly characteristic use of colour. Another Chicago artist was Will Carqueville who produced a number of posters for Lippincott the publisher, while over in Boston the *Daily Herald* commissioned an advertisement from Ethel Reded the first American woman artist to gain a reputation as a poster designer. Edwin Austin Abbey, one of the most renowned American artists of his time, followed the example of English and French academic artists by producing a poster design. Among his best-known works were the series of wall paintings he did for the Boston Public Library on the quest for the Holy Grail and he also devoted an illustrated book to this theme. The poster he designed to promote it was a distinguished piece of work but has a somewhat ponderous quality. The finest American achievements in poster design were works by younger artists.

The poster artist worked either for an advertiser, or, more probably, for a printer. In the second case the copyright remained with the printer who might or might not permit the artist's signature to appear on the finished product. For example Waterlow and Sons held the copyright on some of Dudley Hardy's productions, while David Allen and Sons employed Albert Morrow and John Hassall. They printed Hassall's famous series for Colman's Mustard. Not unnaturally the artists tended to be somewhat bitter about those printers who refused to allow their names to appear on the poster but they had plenty of other complaints, most of them directed against the advertisers.

The minor designer Will True relates a telling anecdote of one advertiser: "I once did a sketch in which a number of white shirt fronts were displayed leaving the paper, as white as any shirt front, untouched. The advertiser was livid: 'If you think I'm going to pay three shillings a poster for white paper you're mistaken, put some pink on 'em.'" It was generally agreed among the artists that advertisers thought they knew more about poster design than the artists themselves and in an interview with the *Poster* magazine John Hassall expanded the point. "The buyers (i.e. the advertisers) are often responsible for a great deal of the bad work seen on the hoardings. They are particularly fond of having a figure shifted to the utter destruction of the composition." Original designs were apparently difficult to sell because the average advertiser rejected out of hand anything in a style that he had not already seen; not so much because of any philistine lack of taste but mainly through an inability to visualize the finished design in its final enlarged state. Hassall believed that the art of the poster was not fully understood in England, but the tradition of which he was one of the founders was to flourish in the next century and England was to take a leading place in the development of poster art throughout Europe.

7
STUNTS AND SHOWMEN

There was very little that the Victorian advertiser could learn from his modern equivalent when it came to the sensational publicity stunt. In an age when the Soldiers of the Queen were viewed with patriotic if sentimental fervour, advertisers did not hesitate to put their sandwich men in the uniforms of well-known regiments while "staff officers" could be seen in London's streets handing out advertising literature. Eventually, in 1894 Parliament was obliged to pass a Uniforms Bill making it unlawful for any but members of the armed forces to wear service uniforms. To some this must have seemed the last straw but the Victorian advertiser was still learning much from his American colleagues. At the end of the century an American food company rented space on the white cliffs of Dover. The grotesque monument they constructed to advertise their product could only be removed after the town council had succeeded in pushing a special bill through Parliament, and many other town councils were obliged to resort to similar measures to fend off the excesses of British private "enterprise" and the "liberty of the individual".

In a letter to *The Times* for October 1900, in which he commented on the rape of Dover's cliffs, Richardson Evans, secretary of the Society for the Checking of Abuses in Public Advertising, wrote: "We ought perhaps to regard with a sense of resentful gratitude the feat of this remote Chicago firm in demonstrating to what lengths in the absence of rational restraint the instinct of vulgar competition can go in affronting the public eye." In an age when even cyclists were accused of defiling the countryside there were, perhaps, some people who were somewhat oversensitive to the dangers of spoiling the environment. But in this case Mr Evans had a point. It was not one shared by the most enthusiastic members of the business community. Ayers Company of Lowell, Mass., makers of the famous Sarsaparilla, appear to have been consumed with regret even at the missed opportunities in pre-Columbian America. Their artist showed Columbus and his intrepid officers looking towards the newly discovered shoreline which could be seen groaning under the weight of massive gantries carrying the name of AYER'S in proud capitals.

This was "creative" thinking indeed, yet the prize for the most imaginative ideas must surely go to two Englishmen. In a delightful illustration from his publication *Successful Advertising* Thomas Smith shows himself asleep on his couch, dreaming seraphic dreams. The picture is captioned "The Advertiser's Vision" and what a vision it was, for there in the clouds above his head floats the dome of St Paul's adorned with the thrilling words: "SMITH'S AGENCY IS THE BEST." "For all sad words of tongue or pen the saddest are these: It might have been." Of course it still might be. St Paul's, unable, it appears, to stand on its own feet, is currently in danger of collapsing. What better way to raise the £3 million required for repairs than to let the dome as a massive hoarding? But this is mere speculation. When in the 1860s Thomas Holloway succeeded in attaching the name of his pills to the Great Pyramid itself, commercial enterprise reached heights which will surely never be surpassed!

In 1885, the university boat race between Oxford and Cambridge was an occasion of even higher drama than usual thanks to the activities of the Waterbury Watch company of America. Determined to make a splash (a pun that must have been heavily overworked during the planning) they arranged an outrageous publicity stunt. Before the race began a steam launch was to be seen proudly cruising at the head of the course, and mounted on it was a figure of Old Father Time holding a Waterbury watch aloft for all to see. Without warning the river banks were suddenly covered with a snowfall of little parcels which on inspection turned out to contain chocolates, sweets and, for the lucky, gift vouchers for Waterbury watches. The heroes of the day were left to their own devices as the crowds converged on the scene to take advantage of this unexpected largesse. In the event, the police had to be called in to control the rush.

As a result of this stunt, Alfred Austin, later the poet laureate, wrote a poem for the Society for the Checking of Abuses in Public Advertising, in which he posed the classic query "Is nothing sacred?" In the March of 1885 this question must have been echoed by hundreds of old Oxford and Cambridge blues and other sportsmen of mature years. The answer, repeated time and time again over the ensuing years to the sound of rattling cash registers and helpless protesters, was "No!" For the sporting world the message must have been driven home once and for all when the great Dr W. G. Grace, the doyen of English cricket, retired from the presidency of the Gloucestershire Cricket Club after a dispute with the Club as to the suitability of advertising on the ground.

Accounts of stunts similar to the boat race event abound, but nowhere do they come bigger and bolder than in the United States, home of free enterprise. In Detroit men thought big even before the arrival of the automobile.

At the time the largest clothing store in Detroit was owned by Mr Mably while the biggest event of the decade was the appearance of Adelina Patti the world famous coloratura soprano. On the day booking started Mably was the first man at the box office. When it opened he demanded of a somewhat dazed booking clerk, "How much the whole theatre?" The man totted it up to about ten thousand dollars whereupon Mably put down the cash and walked off with every seat in the house at his disposal. To all subsequent enquiries the clerk had the same answer: "Mr Mably has bought the house, you must apply to him." The clothier refused to sell and instead gave every ticket away, thus, in the words of a contemporary, "becoming more talked about than even Patti herself!"

For the alert advertising man there was no situation where selling was not possible and where publicity could not be improved. And the really alert advertising men did tend to be in America. A leading shoe shop on Broadway doubled its sales one week by exhibiting a display of Indian moccasins in its windows. Crowds of interested spectators gathered in front of this sidewalk museum and few left without first going into the shop for expert explanation of the method of manufacture, tribal styles and other points of academic interest. In most cases, the practical outcome of this healthy curiosity was also a new and, on mature reflection, unwanted pair of shoes. Betrayed by footwear retailers, New Yorkers also found themselves pestered by their barbers. Of course this affliction has not been confined to the citizens of New York in the 1890s; but those were the days when many men went to the barber for their shave. Thus the customer might find himself playing captive audience every day, with the added disadvantage of having a razor at his throat if he showed the slightest signs of flagging interest. To all this was added a new torment when barbers began renting the ceilings of their shops for the use of advertisers.

The greatest showman of them all was Phineas Taylor Barnum. He began in business at the age of twenty-five in 1835 by exhibiting the aged slave Joyce Heth whom he claimed was 161 years old and had been the nurse of George Washington. Whether she was what he said Barnum made enough out of her before she died the following year to persuade himself that his future lay in showmanship. His next venture, held at the American Museum in New York, gave him a nation-wide reputation. Here the enquirer could see the Fiji Mermaid, fabricated by a skilful taxidermist from the upper half of a monkey and the lower half of a fish; "the original" Siamese twins and, most famous of all, the dwarf Tom Thumb who never achieved a greater height than thirty-three inches and died, at the age of forty-five, rich and famous having been entertained by President Lincoln. Barnum himself retired at the age of forty-five to invest the huge profits he had made, but the only result was bankruptcy and in 1871 he was obliged to launch the "Greatest Show On Earth" which became ten years later the world famous Barnum and Bailey's circus.

Because of his phenomenal success Barnum's pronouncements on the subject of advertising and publicity naturally had considerable currency and the brash showman became one of the pillars of the advertising establishment. Anything that attracted and held the interest of his public was grist to Barnum's mill, and his public was every man, woman and child in the land. One day citizens of New York whose business took them near Barnum's museum were fascinated by the doings of a down-at-heel tramp who seemed to be having problems with bricks. What was happening was far from clear; what the man did was as follows. First he placed each of his five bricks at a busy road-crossing, then squaring his shoulders and stepping out briskly, he began marching from one to the other, occasionally changing their positions as though to satisfy the specifications of some predetermined plan. What this plan was he refused to disclose and within an hour he had an audience of hundreds; at the end of the hour the "brick layer" turned smartly into Barnum's Museum to be followed by a score or so of the more insatiably curious of his spectators. For a week or more the man earned his dollar a day and before the police at last put a stop to it Barnum had increased his take by considerably more. This kind of thing yielded an immediate return, but it also earned many column inches of free publicity in the news pages. Barely a week went past without some sensation with the elements of a good story. Barnum made news and the newspapers helped to make Barnum. In 1850 he turned to a more "respectable" line of show business when he promoted the tour of the singer Jenny Lind, the so-called Swedish Nightingale. Barnum changed his style, but not much – engravings on the covers of the sheet music published for the tour show the famous singer being greeted by the impressario, given equal prominence. "Advertising," said Barnum, "is like learning; a little is a bad thing." He was to be enthusiastically echoed by agents on both sides of the Atlantic many times before the end of the century.

Barnum's promotions seemed spectacular in their own right – this was half his success. There were plenty of fairground showmen round the country with displays no less *outré* but when the fakes and freaks were presented by Barnum somehow they really did seem remarkable phenomena. Just how difficult it could be to make the unusual appear sensational is revealed by the hilarious story of the strong man Eugene Shadow. Of German extraction he came to England where he built up a satisfactory reputation as the strongest man of the day and had opened a number of schools of "physical culture". In 1890 he struck on a new and startling stunt which was to lift a full grown horse with one hand. At this stage he was concerned only with promotional material and accordingly "communicated his idea to the printers Messrs Allen and Son with a view to having it presented in a large picture". Three years later the stunt had still to be performed and the printers had written to Mr Shadow asking him to remove his posters from their warehouse. According to Shadow the printers were persuaded to store them longer for a fee and the following year he organized a tour in the course of which he was at last to hold up a full grown horse. Accordingly he dispatched a request for posters, and to his horrified indignation the printers replied that they had sold the entire stock to Messrs Murphy of Dublin, Brewers, who were now using them to advertise the strength of their stout.

There were other stunts which went wrong. In America Dr Henry T. Hembold, a New York druggist, not unreasonably as he thought, wanted to cash in on national disaster to make his millions. With a military skill that was clearly wasted he calculated the day on which Richmond, Virginia would fall to the Northern troops and offered one thousand dollars for a full page in the *New York Herald* of that day, 5 April 1865. His foresight was impeccable and his offer was entirely reasonable, but he fell a victim to the principles of an editor. Mr Hembold had reasoned that when this the last great victory had been won, people in their thousands would buy the *Herald* and that any advertiser who controlled a whole page of the paper on that day could not fail to attract the attention of the public. Yet for James Gordon Bennet, the publisher of the *Herald*, even $1,000 was not enough, because, as he said, he needed all the pages at his disposal to tell the story of the historic victory. In his defeat Hembold no doubt consoled himself with the fact that the name of his product, in the words of a contemporary, was to be found on "every dead wall, fence, rock and telegraph pole from the Atlantic to the Pacific".

If the English were prepared to learn the arcane mysteries of publicity from almost any American, the Americans were continually delighted by the doings of the big bad men of advertising. Nothing was beyond the pale if the results were cheap promotion and even the sacred precepts of "good neighbourliness" were neglected if there was a chance for a profitable bit of deception. With considerable relish the *Evening Sun* of Wilmington, Delaware, told the following tale of commercial rivalry that dominated the gossip of 1899.

It all began when the store keeper Herbert Watson decided on a thorough renovation of his premises. It seemed to him that the time was ripe for a new image. Accordingly he commissioned estimates for redecorating the outside and inside of the store, for moving the counter and building new shelves, for shifting a door here and changing a wall there and generally set things in train for something of a face lift. Now Herbie had never reckoned himself artistic and he was just as pleased as could be when Col. A. L. Ainsworth, late of the United States Cavalry and owner of the restaurant across the road, came over to see how things were shaping up. The Colonel made a number of fine suggestions and most of all he urged Herbie to get himself a splendid new crystal glass wall mirror. The opinion was backed up by others and although it cost him more than somewhat, Herbie got out his roll and bought the finest wall mirror that Wilmington ever had seen.

The alterations were judged a success by one and all and especially by the colonel who would drop in twice a week as regular as clockwork to sit at his neighbour's soda bar and look with delight and also unaccountable amusement at the new mirror. He never stayed for long and usually left his glass of soda unfinished on the counter, but after these visits, Herb couldn't help noticing, all the customers at the bar seemed to be sharing Ainsworth's joke. It was something of a mystery but our storeman didn't bother himself unduly until one day noticing a mark on the beautiful glass he turned round cloth in hand to give it a polish. And now he could see what his customers could see – every time they came in for a soda. There, beautifully framed by the mirror, was the shop front of Ainsworth's restaurant on the opposite side of the street, dishes temptingly displayed in the window and the day's special menu clearly legible in large capital letters – all done in mirror writing. The inartistic Mr Watson was lost in admiration at the man's ingenuity and harboured no grudges. He was after all a practical fellow and started proceedings to recover $11,400 dollars in damages; considering this a fair rental for a year's free publicity.

Willing to be impressed by the bigness of everything American, the agents of the late Victorian period sometimes forgot the heroic struggles of the pioneers in England. The Great Exhibition, held in 1851, was alone the most sensational publicity exercise of the century and was eagerly seized on by British manufacturers to be exploited for their own ends. John Bennett, a watch and clock manufacturer, acquired the back page of the catalogue for the phenomenal sum of 1,000 guineas (something like £15,000 in modern money). Half a million copies had been printed for sale at the Exhibition and to be used as promotional material and Bennett was quite content with what he considered to be something of a bargain. One can imagine his fury on learning that the publishers had sold half the total print run (250,000 copies) to Mappin's the cutlery firm of Sheffield who had thereupon had them bound in red cloth, embossed in gold-tooling with their own name, trademark and advertisements. Bennett took Mappin's to court but to no effect, the judge ruling that the defendants had a perfect right to bind the books, which were after all their property, whatever might be printed on the back page. In fact, as he admitted several years and a knighthood later, Bennett made a handsome profit on orders from the advertisement; not the least being one which came in from Siam fifteen years after the Great Exhibition for a 125 guinea chronometer. "The pattern was out of date," Sir John observed to his interviewer, "but I soon faked one up and sent it off. I remember that we got a letter of thanks afterwards."

Another Englishman achieved a still more sensational success. His name remains cloaked in mystery yet the account of his legendary deed is vouched for by the American journal *Printers' Ink*. The story is set in Calcutta where a dangerous criminal was preparing for his execution. The preliminaries had just about been completed when an Englishman, who had recently arrived and had heard of the impending spectacle, pushed his way through the crowds to request permission to speak with the condemned man. They were together about five minutes and as the Englishman left the criminal shouted after him: "Never forget that you promised a thousand pounds to my heirs." The convicted man was then led to the scaffold where he begged the customary right to make his farewell speech. This being granted he roared aloud to the assembled multitude: "All you who listen, hear my dying statement: the best coffee is the coffee of Messrs Chicory, Chewem and Chocker, of Calcutta and London!" The company's identity is concealed by printers' ink.

One year the citizens of King William IV's London were surprised to see a top hat some eight foot high being drawn through the streets by a horse. The only sign of the driver was his whip projecting a few feet up from the brim and the sole function of this unique conveyance was to notify passers-by of the address of Mr Perring, inventor and hat maker. In fact, Perring felt hard done by. In 1827 he had introduced "hats by weight", but "numerous contemporaries had set up in the neighbourhood and elsewhere professing the greatest absurdities as regards the weight and price of hats so that unless some attention was paid to the address the purchaser was likely to obtain a mere copy for an original". Perring claimed: "A LIGHT HAT is of the greatest importance to the studious; it allows our ideas to expand and prevents depression of the spirits." Any contemporary who could devise a greater absurdity deserved, one can't help thinking, all the sales he could get. Yet Mr Perring's imitators would stop at nothing and some even went so far as to display a pair of scales in the window, as he did, to drive home the message of weight. The end result, as Perring records in one of his hand bills, was that he was obliged to build a HAT UPON WHEELS (cost sixty guineas, or so he claimed) which was to be seen "perambulating the town daily, reminding the observer where good cheap hats may be bought, at Cecil House, 85 The Strand".

Among the incensed Londoners who saw Perring's contraption was Thomas Carlyle who was so outraged that he felt obliged to comment on it in *Past and Present*. Unaware of the injustices that drove the hatter to this last desperate expedient he heaped abuse on the man: "He has not attempted to make better hats, as he was appointed by the Universe to do, . . . but his whole industry is turned to *persuade* us that he has made such! He too, knows that the Quack has become God." Far from it! Mr Perring, ignorant of the cosmic obligation laid on him to make better hats, was simply attempting to sell as many as possible of the ones he did make. It is surely a poignant comment on the uphill battle fought by the nineteenth-century advertiser that even the universe was invoked against him.

However, there were those among Perring's contemporaries who disdained to compete with him. Aldard's of High Holborn did base their reputation on quality rather than cheapness and their advertising followed a more conventional path. A line-drawing shows Mr Dandy at the cloakroom to collect his hat from the waiter; but he is in for a nasty shock.

Mr Dandy "That is not my hat. Mine is a capital good one!"
Tom Handy (the waiter) "Very sorry, Sir! But all the best hats have been gone this half hour."
Mr Dandy "Well! But I can't wear that, it is such a shocking bad hat – what am I to do?"
Tom Handy "Well Sir, if I might take the liberty to advise, I would recommend your going to ALDARD'S, 120 HIGH HOLBORN."

Another businessman to outrage the proprieties and raise the blood pressures of the establishment seems to have been Mr Frederick Marriott who, like the dreadful Perring, also hailed from the Strand. The advertising van had long been popular and was to remain a common mode of publicity until the end of the century, contributing materially to the traffic jams which then as now were a habitual feature of the London scene. Mr Marriott had a variation on the idea. In 1845 he registered, as an article of utility, a "public omnibus". Since their introduction in 1829 these vehicles had carried advertisements on the outside, but the notion of advertising inside brought on apoplexies even in the editorial offices of *Punch*. "Do in mercy allow us to ride for a day's pleasure to the Bank to receive our dividends, without compelling us to sit *vis à vis* to Moses and Son, or having Rowland's Kalydor perpetually thrown in our faces. Let us be a nation of shopkeepers as much as we please but there is no necessity that we should become a nation of advertisers." But these views were not everyone's. *Punch*'s contributor Douglas Jerrold does not seem to have been particularly disturbed at the prospect and commented aptly that by Marriott's proposal the advertising vans would be turned outside in.

The idea that advertising was separate from the real concerns of commerce and that shopkeepers need not be advertisers was the general view in Britain and explains the unremitting campaigning by agents to persuade companies to advertise. By the end of the century they had made considerable progress but were still eager to concede the American lead in the field to spur their English clients to still greater efforts.

In an article for the *Windsor Magazine* of February 1900, entitled "How Americans Advertise", F. Klickman was abject in his admiration of American achievements in the field. "In England we speak with bated breath of the stupendous power that advertising has achieved in our midst. Yet despite the artistic character of our posters and the 101 novel devices to which the modern advertiser resorts it is a prosaic fact that we are still but guileless babes in our handling of the matter when compared with our relatives overseas." But he overstated the case. The English were capable of real stuntmanship by the end of the century, both on their own account and on behalf of American companies if employed by them.

In the last month of the century Charing Cross Road, London was the scene of events that would not disgrace the pages of P. G. Wodehouse; indeed to judge from his name the defence barrister must have walked straight out of them. The hearing was at the Marlborough Street Police Court and the defendants, R. C. Wyatt, A. Simpson Slater and James Hough of the Edison Bell Consolidated Phonograph Company. These bright young fellows, who had entrusted their defence to none other than Mr Bodkin, were faced by the solid form of Inspector Tuckett glowering at them from the witness box. At 6.30 p.m. he had been proceeding down the Charing Cross Road in a southerly direction when his attention was attracted by a crowd of about a thousand persons gathered outside the building that housed the offices of the company. The cause of the assembly was evidently the phonographic machine in the window of a first floor room. "The machine played several patriotic songs, such as *Soldiers of the Queen* and *Rule Britannia* and the crowd became very patriotic, and took off their hats and waved them in the air, as they also did their walking sticks."

By a happy coincidence it was the opening night of Mr Wyndham's new theatre opposite the offices of the company and what the inspector described as "great excitement" was caused. This merely in passing; for Tuckett was a hard man and forcing his way through a thousand stick waving patriots he effected an entrance into the offices of the said company. When he demanded that the disturbance be stopped, Wyatt, one of the directors, eagerly inquired into the possibility of a summons which, he opined, would be a "splendid advertisement". In any case he refused to stop playing his gramophone and the performance continued until nine o'clock, while down below Inspector

Tuckett and thirty constables endeavoured to control the traffic and keep the people moving. Unwisely a "portion" of the phonograph had been allowed to project a few inches out of the window and could thus be technically construed as outside the premises. Accordingly the defendants were ordered to pay six shillings for the withdrawal of the summons and, after a few friendly words from the judge, who was obviously fascinated by the whole episode, left the court as free and very cheaply-advertised men.

In the fight for sales manufacturers and tradesmen resorted to any and every device. One weekly newspaper issued thousands of pennies overstamped with its name, and when Parliament passed a special act suppressing this kind of defacement of the coinage they lost several thousand pounds in withdrawing the offending coins and returning them to the Mint. Other advertisers simply stencilled their messages on pavements and streets and one entrepreneur erected a number of glass pillars at strategic sites in London, among them Hyde Park Corner, which he rented out for bill sticking. The effect must have been very similar to the pillars used in Paris and if generally adopted would have done something to lessen the scourge of "fly posting". In the event it was the abolition of tax on advertisements that reduced the need for indiscriminate bill sticking. While the tax had been in force the practice had appealed to advertisers since posters were not taxed, as a result they had been plastered over every available wall space in London by an army of bill posters who respected nothing and feared no one. The menace reached its height during the 1830s and 1840s and eventually a bill of Parliament was passed making it illegal to stick posters on a property without the owner's permission. The bill had little effect; offices, private houses and derelict properties were covered time and again with a kind of *al fresco* wallpaper. Between themselves the fly posters observed one point of honour – they waited till paste had dried on their rival's poster before superimposing their own. The result of continual overpasting was that strange and garbled messages made their appearance on the walls. "Madame Vestris having recovered from her severe indisposition will appear this evening in THE POWERFUL AND MAGNIFICENT STEAM SHIP 'FAVOURITE' 210 HORSEPOWER" is a comparatively mild example and this genre of mistaken messages was a favourite source for the "humorous papers" of the time. From the 1850s a degree of order was imposed on the situation as powerful bill posting companies began to buy up hoardings and enforce their claim to let space on them. During the great days, the profession of free lance bill sticker had been a profitable one, even if the occasional pitched battles between rival gangs introduced an element of danger.

The first man to make real capital out of leasing advertising space was James Willing. He started business in 1842 with the simple but effective idea of exploiting toll gates as points of advertising; since travellers were obliged to stop at the gate they were ideal for his purpose and as he offered to rent the space from the toll-keepers they made it their business to protect the space from rival bill stickers. Soon Mr Willing's "protected advertising spaces" were known throughout the country and Willing's Hoardings were a household word by the end of the century.

To his stationary hoardings James Willing added a fleet of advertising vans and the company's business, not only in posters but in the whole field of advertising, prospered so well that Willing arranged the publicity for Barnum's visit to England. In 1874 Willing's *Press Guide* made its first appearance and today the company, still among London's leading agents, is also one of the oldest.

8
THE ARTS OF THE COPYWRITER

An article in *Ainsworth's Magazine* for July 1842 gave an analysis of the techniques used by publishers to promote book sales. The writer dealt not with advertisements as such but rather with what can best be called a public relations exercise. First came the "puff preliminary" which was a straightforward "rave" review. It was followed by the puff negative: "It is not true that the talented author of *FitzHenry Fitz Hildebrand* has disposed of the copyright of that charming work to the publisher for £1,000 nor is it a fact that the duel fought the day before yesterday at Wimbledon had any connexion with these witty volumes." Then there came the puff mysterious:

> It has been hinted that a certain noble duke . . . has been unable to conceal from himself that certain passages in the new novel bear reference to himself; and that some of them are calculated to cause a ruption with the beautiful and fascinating Contessa to whom he has been so long devoted and who had hitherto flattered herself that the details of her *liaison* with his grace had been a profound secret. It would be well if a certain lordling who resides not a hundred miles from Grosvenor Square, and who has also sat for his picture in this literary picture gallery, were to profit by the witty and caustic lessons of the author.

Later, if sales still needed a boost, a puff deprecatory was launched on a punch drunk public: "Looking like the spontaneous sentiment of the editor of the journal in which it appears it is done to order by the square foot, like its predecessors, the editor, in reality, having as little interest in the fate of the book as though it had never been written."

> We sincerely trust, that the public will not suffer its mind to be biassed by the report now current that the novel entitled *FitzHenry Fitz Hildebrand* which has excited so great and so universal a sensation in the most distinguished circles is not the production of its reputed author but that they will read the work and judge fairly for themselves. All we have to say on the subject is that if it be not written by our old favourite, another literary Brutus has risen who will make even him look to his laurels.

Book publishers were among the first to employ advertising on a large scale, together with the merchants of patent medicines, and their "puffs" gave a new name to the English language. If, in the words of Dr Johnson, advertisement is "Promise, large promise" the book puff promised a new genius with every publication date. Compared with the methods of mid-century advertising their techniques appear almost refined but their methods, if indirect, were effective. Later, advertising agents were to canvas new clients with the alluring promise that they could so convince editors and lecturers of the virtues of any important new invention that it would receive notice in the news columns of the press with all the authority of the journal itself. The procedure had been pioneered generations back by the booksellers; it is possible that it is with us yet.

The level of copywriting was not high at first but elementary lessons were being learned even as early as the 1850s. When they first introduced their services to the public the proprietors of Professor Browne's Celebrated Hair Cutting Saloons of 47 Fenchurch Street, made a big selling point out of their equally "celebrated Scurf Brushes". It is a common misconception about the Victorians that they were constitutionally unable to call a spade a spade. Professor Browne had no such inhibitions; nevertheless, perhaps on the kindly advice of a friend, he did come to change his approach and in later advertisements dropped all reference to the special qualities of these celebrated pieces of equipment in favour of a simple statement that "a clean pair of brushes is used to every person".

By the end of the reign copywriting had got much more sophisticated thanks in large measure to the propaganda of the agents. Most sizeable agencies employed a full-time body of copywriters by 1900. Even in the

1880s, if few agents employed a staff of writers many were aware of the special requirements of the art and contracted their writing out to freelance specialists.

Agents like Collins were continually boasting of their contacts with literary gentlemen and such freelance copywriters occasionally advertised in the professional press. But although the English were realizing that this branch of the literary art was a specialist occupation the fees were still modest; ten shillings for the average "small ad" was considered fair by both parties. It was with astonished envy that the English "expert ad-writer" read of the kind of money that his American opposite numbers could make. One wonders what a London advertiser of the period would have said if presented with a bill for £200 for a three-inch single column piece of copy, yet this was paid by an American manufacturer who thought his money well spent. English ad. writers enviously took note of the fact.

At this time the Americans seem to have had an almost religious awe of the power of advertising. The columns of the press were peppered with astonishing tales of instant fortunes owed entirely to advertisement and of firms forced to call a halt to their campaigns while they battled against floods of orders that threatened to overwhelm them entirely. One of the most renowned of the copywriters, George Augustus Sala, once said that he would rather tackle a three volume novel than an advertising booklet. No one could accuse these "ad-smiths" – the term they modestly adopted – of selling themselves short, and what would have been the point. A man who had just spent, in today's prices, about £2,000 on a three-inch small ad would be only too happy to learn that his purchase was placed by sound judges in the same category as the works of William James. And if a copywriter sold himself short what use could he be expected to be in selling someone else?

Mr Gladstone is known to have turned to the advertising pages of the American press when in need of diversion and there, in the year 1886, he might have seen the notice published by the *Solid Muldoon* of Colorado. In those days the state of Colorado had by no means forgotten the sturdy traditions of its frontier past and the *Solid Muldoon*, describing itself as the "Boss Paper", was appealing to a type of readership rarely, if ever, catered for in England. It was, it claimed, "The only fearless wide awake and red hot newspaper published in San Juan. Democratic in politics; independent in development; and no religion worth speaking of. She's a daisy." It is pleasant to imagine the austere Gladstone, after perhaps a particularly gruelling encounter with the Queen, regaling himself in the privacy of his home with this kind of subversive literature.

Unquestionably it had punch; but it lacked the new style introduced to American copywriting by John E. Powers. Called "the father of honest advertising", he had been a copywriter and publicity adviser to Wanamaker's Stores of Philadelphia and had acted as consultant to a number of other firms. Powers started two new lines of approach to advertising copy in the 1880s: first he insisted on giving an honest message; second he introduced a simple straightforward style of English that dispensed entirely with the kind of wild exaggeration that had been the stock in trade of advertisements before him.

With somewhat surprised condescension an English observer, writing at the end of the century for a lay audience, explained that "Wanamakers of Philadelphia gives a liberal salary to an expert whose sole occupation is to turn out naive productions by the yard." But Powers' honest style soon attracted emulation in England. One of these was probably C. A. G. Browne who set up an agency in 1895 and made it a basic principle to accept only those accounts that could be promoted honestly.

It must have been surprising to even the most enthusiastic English agents to find just how seriously their American colleagues viewed copywriting. The *Advertisers' Review* for 5 June 1899 carried a quotation from the *Chicago Herald* to stir the imagination. "The latest school to teach a profession, it began, is the College of Advertising." The planned curriculum was certainly comprehensive and included composition, the use of words, type, display lithography, paper, rates and space. Students were given a practical as well as a theoretical grounding by visits to newspaper offices and printing works, and despite the semi-academic status they had given to their profession, the founders were anxious to dispel the impression that, "advertising is necessarily surrounded by a halo of mystery". In fact they claimed that advertising was now a business science and as a science was capable of being taught. Within two months of opening the doors they had nineteen enrolments and considered this sufficiently encouraging to turn what had been an experimental venture into a going concern.

Denied the advantage of a professional training, the writers of Rowland's copy nevertheless had a sense of occasion. In the New Year of 1838 they adopted their most unctious tones to celebrate the anniversary of the young Queen's reign. "A New Year is an epoch in our lives that forms an interesting subject for reflection to the millions who people the civilized globe. But by none perhaps is the birth of another child of Time hailed with fonder enthusiasm than by the happy subjects of this realm." As the years passed and the novelty of a girl queen gave way to the routine of Victorian prosperity the approach becomes more general but the sense of occasion is retained as the makers of these elegant toilet requisites work their way through the year. During the London Season, Rowland's Macassar Oil is indispensable to all who "court the GAY and FESTIVE SCENES especially during the Dance or the heated atmosphere of crowded assemblies". As summer approaches the ballroom gives place to the "Fashionable Promenade", "the RIDE, and DRIVE and the recurrence of the summer solstice invites the full display of FEMALE BEAUTY". But dangers lurk and Kalydor, an excellent lotion for the skin, comes into its own, "neutralizing the effects produced by temporary exposure to solar heat upon the neck, arms and face". At the height of summer the advertisement for July carries a still graver warning to ladies visiting the seaside. "The heat of summer also frequently communicates a dryness to the hair and a tendency to FALL OFF, which may be completely obviated by the use of Macassar oil." And then as the festive season rolls round again the use of Rowland's Auxiliaries to health and beauty become once more unusually essential. It was a full calendar which could be carried through with confidence only with the help of Messrs Rowland's preparations.

Such laboured urbanity was rarely equalled by other English advertisers (perhaps we should be grateful for the fact) but who can doubt that the proprietors of the Laong Chung Hsi Tea Shop, with the riches of their native Mandarin at their disposal, exercised the arts of persuasion with a still more telling elegance. Something of the style communicates itself even in the intriguing ad., prepared by their translator for the export market. "I wish to the tea shop from first at Fookien the there have mountaing of nome is Whoo Lee that, tea tree is from aionside the country the tea and out small of belong superid perhaps it is of greut value if have inferiro sample that another port, or another hows. has of thank very much to do patronize for me long tame. that have would use me man is five whare now. please to yonllook of this rill for prioe true."

This kind of thing can have had only a limited appeal. Most advertisers went for the direct approach. "When you ask for GLENFIELD starch see that you get it, as inferior kinds are often substituted for the sake of higher profits" or "Paint your own bath with Griffiths Vitros of Liquid Porcelain. Stands boiling water."

At the end of the century *Printers' Ink* was urging that the merchant should supervise or write his own advertisements so that they would show his personality and not that of some expert such as Gillam or Powers, but in England agents were still pressing the older view that advertisement writers were born and not made. In their opinion the wise merchant went to an agent when he wanted copy written, but they could not hope to resist such a manufacturer as J. C. Eno with his intensive approach to publicity.

Eno's rarely took less than half a page, not so much because of any theoretical commitment to display advertising but simply to accommodate the vast amount of copy, extensive even by Victorian standards. During the 1880s and 1890s the inside cover of Cassell's *Family Magazine* was dominated week after week by the names of Fry's and Eno's divided by merely a printers' rule, though the contrast in layout and copy was dramatic. Never taking more than the top quarter of the page the cocoa company was content to present the simple message of its name and product, making good use of large display type and with the additional attraction of an engraving. Up to the end of the 1880s this usually showed a "View of the Manufactory, Bristol" – a favourite topic for illustration with capitalists of the high Victorian period, who were unaccountably proud of their dark Satanic mills. In the 1890s the public was treated to a tray of cocoa, complete with steaming cups and a tin of the powder.

The Victorians were probably more impressed with the offerings of the indefatigable and socially involved Mr Eno. Working in a century old tradition of patent medicine he was governed, in any case, by different conventions; moreover he was selling a specific meant to ease constipation or to cure the liverish complaints of over-indulgence in food and drink. Both were familiar enough topics to the Victorians who saw nothing untoward in the philosophizing and moralizing that filled an Eno's ad. Eno was not short of the indispensable testimonials for his product but he also used valuable space to advise on the principles of healthy living, advice which if followed would have killed the market for his product. One of the regular features of his ads were the seven "HEALTH MAXIMS" by which, apparently, dyspepsia could be cured. Three meals a day, "not an atom between meals" and the cutting up of all animal food into pea sized pieces, to be well chewed. The instructions conclude with a quotation from "J.C.E." himself proposing a diet of oysters and fresh lemon juice. It is however a fact, and for medicine manufacturers a profitable one, that people do not heed good advice.

Elsewhere we read about attacks of "mild dysentery and billiousness" suffered in foreign parts by the pioneers of empire and brought on by "ill-considered devotion to brandy".

The empire indeed, seems to have been maintained by soldiers and administrators invigorated and supported in every conceivable and inconceivable way by the miraculous fruit salt. Commander A. J. Loftus, His Siamese Majesty's hydrographer, never went into the jungle without a tin. During four years of important survey expeditions in the Malay peninsula, Siam and Cambodia he recorded only one instance when a member of the party was attacked by fever – "and that happened after our supply of FRUIT SALT ran out". Fortified by generations of oriental wisdom the Siamese resisted the remarkable powers of this effervescent magic, achieved by the dextrous admixture of Sodium Bicarbonate, Tartaric Acid and Anydrous Citric Acid. The Masai of Kenya were not so lucky and at the hands of the white medicine man, Joseph Thomson, F.R.G.S., they got the full treatment.

> A medicine also had to be prepared for the disease, which I did by laying out a small medicine-box, with the lid open, showing all the array of phials, etc. Taking out my sextant, and putting on a pair of kid gloves – which accidently I happened to have and which impressed the natives enormously, I intently examined the contents. Discovering the proper *dawa*, I prepared a mixture and getting ready some ENO'S FRUIT SALT, I sang an incantation – in general something about "Three Blue Bottles" – over it. My voice not being astonishingly mellifluous it did duty capitally for a wizard's. My preparations complete, and Brahim being ready with a gun, I dropped the Salt into the mixture; simultaneously the gun was fired and, lo! up fizzed and sparkled the carbonic acid . . . the chiefs with fear and trembling taste as it fizzes away.

The naivete of the untutored black was of course always good for a laugh to the Victorians but Thomson's display must have made pretty impressive viewing for people who had never seen even fizzy lemonade. More amusing is the naivete of the manufacturer, the point of the story being of course that to persuade the Masai to take his unfamiliar remedies, Thomson laid on a show in which the famous fruit salt provided only the "magic" effects. But Eno seems to have been innocent of a sense of humour. Under the flaming headline HOW KANDAHAR WAS WON we find a quotation from *Mess Stories* by Mr G. W. Vyse: "During the Afghan war I verily believe Kandahar was won by us all taking up large supplies of ENO'S FRUIT SALT and so arrived fit to overthrow half-a-dozen Ayub Khans." In 1888 a bottle was left to do its work in the dark recesses of the Atlas Mountains. In September of that year Mr Harold Chrichton-Browne had been treated so hospitably by the Kaid of Demnet that he and his party desired to make the ruler some acknowledgement. Accordingly they "presented him with a box of Huntley and Palmer's biscuits and a bottle of Eno's Fruit Salts, with which he was much pleased". Mr Browne wrote to tell *The World* newspaper of his generosity but history does not record the sentiments of the Kaid as the magical effervescent powder got to work on his royal stomach.

From Siam to darkest Africa, the world had been forced to acknowledge the superior qualities of Eno's Fruit Salts but none of these testimonials matched the lyricism that inspired the General Officer who wrote from Ascot. "Blessings on your Fruit Salt," he began, "I trust it is not profane to say so, but I swear by it. There stands the cherished bottle on the Chimney piece of my sanctum, my little idol – at home my household god, abroad my vade mecum. Think not this is the rhapsody of a hypochondriac, no! It is only the outpouring of a grateful heart. The fact is, I am, in common with numerous old fellows of my age (67), now and then troubled with a troublesome liver." The truth is out. Here we seem to be confronted with the finest example of a case of "ill-considered devotion to brandy" that one could hope to meet. The poetic General's couplets only confirm the diagnosis.

"When Eno's salt betimes you take
No waste of this elixir make,
But drain the dregs and lick the cup,
Of this the perfect Pick-me-up."

The manufacturers were delighted and adopted "At home my household god, abroad my vade mecum" as a regular slogan thereafter. And with fan mail like this J. C. Eno did not have to look far for promotional copy – he could devote his literary gifts to more important matters. In one advertisement a diatribe against the horrors of war neatly leads into a discussion of the one thing that is more terrible – failure to observe the rules of health and natural hygiene. Another quotes Carlyle to the effect that "The accursed hag dyspepsia had got him bitted and bridled", and yet another quoted Chaucer to somewhat obscure purpose. One theme Eno took especially seriously, because he regarded it as a matter of public urgency, was the subject of city sanitation.

By the 1890s the work of the reformer Edward Chadwick had forced reluctant authorities to tackle the scandalous conditions in Britain's great conurbations. But there was still much to be done and drawing on the writings of Chadwick and others Eno used his advertisements in a campaign of public education that was of real value and importance. As a series his advertisements conform to the Victorian enthusiasm for instruction through entertainment; in retrospect they provide a fascinating prospectus of the interests and concerns of a century ago; and, more to the point, they sold millions of bottles of Eno's Fruit Salts.

Among Eno's rivals was one with a still greater fear of empty space on the page.

> ARE SAVAGES BETTER OFF?
>
> An ex-officer of the German army declares that savages are in better case than civilized men. He wants to found a colony to put his ideas to the test and proposes that these experimental colonists should settle on some convenient Pacific Island. "Under my plan men would have better souls and better stomachs" says this queer German.
>
> We don't know about the souls. As for the stomach . . . the spectacled professors say that from the development of his jaws it is clear that our prehistoric ancestor never had indigestion. But here is the experience of a man of our own day. "For over twenty years I suffered from a bad stomach. In August 1881 I read about a medicine, Mother Seigel's Curative Syrup, . . . I got a bottle from Mr Suttie, High Street, Perth . . . after the second bottle I was cured."
>
> As to the savage tribes having been healthier than we in this age are, the German officer is wholly wrong. History is dead against him. All savage tribes suffer fearfully from dyspepsia!

The anecdotal approach was clearly thought to be a winner by Mother Seigel's copywriter; indeed, the full pages the company were regularly persuaded to invest in were only just big enough to accommodate his novelettes. While some used space for impact – the simple message, the trade name and the pretty picture – Seigel's clearly considered such an approach a criminal waste. Under the heading BREAD AND CAKE, the brand name appears only twice and then in the last two paragraphs of a closely reasoned piece running to some 500 words of close set type. This economic use of space enabled the advertiser to tell the story of Mr William Edwards, a tailor and draper whose doctor had recommended a change of air. The piece had opened with the story of Marie Antoinette who when told that the people were desperate for lack of bread had advised that they eat cake. Like Mr Edward's doctor she was recommending the impossible remedy. To quote the words of the advertisement: "It's odd what links make up the chain of associated ideas, isn't it?"

Testimonials from satisfied users were an essential feature of advertisements for patent medicine in Victorian times. Despite the confident panache with which he presented his astonishing claims the manufacturer was prepared to consider that he might be mistaken. A purveyor of old wives' remedies he operated in an area where gossip was the best recommendation and so he eagerly used the opinions of others to buttress the authority of herbal lore and misrepresented science.

Such testimonials, presented as the authentic voice of the great British public, were used by manufacturers of all sorts of goods during the nineteenth century and were far more common than they are today. It was even better if famous public figures came forward, or could be induced to come forward, to sing the praises of the product.

The manufacturers of Koko hair tonic received a real gem of a testimonial from the famous actress Miss Ellen Terry. To modern readers it has what can only be described as a certain naïve charm, spelling out with engaging frankness just the kind of thing the makers loved to hear. She writes: "I have used KOKO for my hair for years . . . it stops the hair from falling out, promotes growth and eradicates dandruff." Before Hollywood it was the stars of stage and opera that bestowed the accolade on toiletries, and they were eager enough. Ellen Terry was joined by Mrs Langtry and Mr Henry Irving in her endorsement of *Salvine* the scientific dentifrice but she was outdone in this field of commercial sponsorship by Lillie Langtry whose protégés included not only Salvine and Pears Soap but also Mr W. Clarkson, Theatrical and Private Wig Maker. Pears also enjoyed the good opinion of the opera singer Adelina Patti and Mme Marie Roze Mapleson but they never got anything out of them to equal Mrs Langtry's letter to Clarkson's the wig-makers. "Mr Clarkson," it read, "I send a line to say that the three wigs you made me are completely satisfactory and that you are the first wig maker who has been able to suit me."

The good opinion of a famous actress boosted sales, the more so if, like Lillie Langtry, she turned out to be the mistress of the heir apparent. But in the palmy days before the great war a manufacturer had a whole army of princesses, kings and emperors who were ready at a moment's notice to run up a testimonial, or who could, without too much ingenuity, be presented as eager sponsors.

On 25 February 1896 Princess Hohenlohe, of the Prussian family, was impelled to write to the makers of KOKO which, as she put it, "is the very best dressing for the hair I know . . . and is in every way excellent". Even before she had ascended the throne the Princess Victoria had been listed as one of the members of the royal family under whose "patronage" the firm of Rowlands claimed to prosper. She can hardly have objected, being in the distinguished company of their Imperial Majesties the Emperor and Empress of Russia, and the Emperors of Austria and China. And if example nearer home was sought it was readily to hand, for His Grace the Duke of Wellington, the most revered man of his age, had joined with the noblemen and gentlemen of the Melton Mowbray Hunt, not to mention other "distinguished characters", to confer his Patronage on the Absolutorium Razor Strop.

During his life the Prince Consort's reputation, too, had been linked to that of a razor strop – to be absolutely specific Cowvan's Canton Strop or the Quadrilateral Chinese Razor Sharpener. After death his memory was invoked to lend dignity to a patent treatment for the hair. One manufacturer backed his trade card/price list with a coloured engraving of the Albert Memorial. It stands out boldly against a cloudy sky but behind it, in letters now almost beyond decipherment, one can just descry the legend ROSSETTER'S HAIR RESTORER – a kind of ghostly premonition of the sky-writing that went on in the 1920s.

The trouble advertisers took to make their effects earned them a fair measure of ridicule and while some of their critics were shocked by the indignities heaped on the royal family others were simply amused by it. A cartoon published in 1844 shows Prince Albert at his toilet, watched by an admiring wife. She holds a poster for Rowland's Kalydor and Odonto tooth powder; both of which preparations are to be seen on the dressing table. Albert is seen adjusting his cravat (from Hall & Co., Wellington Street the Strand), commenting as he does so "Vates was right: There is an end to a stiff-necked generation, these Albert Elastic Cravats are undescribable things." To which ambiguous comment his queen replies: "They certainly are a wonderful improvement, dear Albert."

As the first man in the kingdom, the Prince inevitably had an influence on the development of fashion. His hatter, Henry Melton, had especial cause to be thankful. "I had patented a shooting hat to combine various advantages – lightness, comfort and availability for all seasons. His Royal Highness, with quick perception, at once recognized these qualifications in the cap and admitted its advantages. His patronage gave a sensational eclat to my patent." This reminiscence comes in a little book *Hints on Hats adapted to the Heads of the People* published by Mr Melton in 1865 just one year after his patron's death. Aware that the sceptical might, to put it bluntly, think he was cashing in on the death of the Prince Consort the court hatter is anxious to silence their carpings. "I beg to assure my readers that I am not actuated by motives chiefly associated with my own interest; my greatest being to offer a humble tribute of gratitude and respect to my illustrious patron, the Prince Consort." As it happened Melton did not need to bother very much what people might say since by now he had gracefully graduated to the post of hatter to the Prince of Wales who "being the 'glass of fashion' must, of course, be followed in suit".

Today the fanfare treatment the Victorian trader gave to his royal or noble patrons has been replaced by the discreet display of the coat of arms and something of the glamour has been lost. Even as Victoria's reign advanced the behaviour, of the classier establishments at least, was becoming a little less boisterous and from the 1870s there were more and more examples of the modern practice of simple display. But if the new custom lost in panache, it may, in one instance, have lost a good deal of trade as well. In 1884 the May issue of the *Sporting Mirror* carried a full page display advertisement for the firm of Joseph Offord, speciality carriage builders. Flanking the maker's name are the arms of His Highness the Viceroy of Egypt and the Emperor of Germany – neither of these illustrious personages would have been happy to know that the captions had been transposed.

For much of her long reign the Queen herself enjoyed notably less respect from her subjects than from posterity. Looking back into that golden time of gunboats and commercial supremacy, latter-day Britons have had their view obscured by the portly figure of a prim little lady. Straight faced and boring, we see her presiding over a world of stuffy bourgeois rectitude, pinning medals, from time to time, on the corsetted torsos of dear soldiers back from planting her flag in another outpost of the empire. Yet the stereotype is about as lifelike as the blurred printer's blocks crouching beside the cheerfully mendacious advertisements of the period. The advertisers themselves certainly had no fears about the penalties for *lèse majesté*; the Queen's portrait was freely used to imply royal associations where none existed. In fact this is one of the few instances in which the picture carried an essential message independent of the words. A portrait of her majesty, cup in hand, about to sample some steaming beverage, was sufficient, together with a manufacturer's name proudly displayed in capital letters, to convince the casual reader that here was the very cocoa drunk whenever crowned heads foregathered. What deductions were to be drawn from the claim that in 1856 Nurse Lilly's ROYAL FEMALE PILLS achieved 20,000 cures, is not clear.

During her declining years the advertising fraternity permitted the Queen to conserve her strength and build up her constitution by imbibing hot chocolate, but as a younger woman she had been obliged to find time in a heavy schedule of state business for proclamations like the following:

PROCLAMATION

Whereas it hath been represented to US, that sundry long and melancholy Faces have been much observed of late, and that others also sadly disposed are still to be seen about Town: Now this, Our Royal Proclamation, is *TO SUMMON* all such to appear at the VICTORIA THEATRE during the run of the Great "GO-A-HEAD" Pantomime; and then and there, to smile, laugh, chuckle, grin, roar, and otherwise cachinnate, and also to apply the palms of their hands frequently and loudly together so as to produce sounds most pleasing to the ear, in order that all Dismals, Dumps, Mumps, Blues and other varieties of Azure Diabolicals may be entirely banished from our Realms and Whomsoever is henceforth, after this Notice, seen and discovered with a visage longer than ordinary, will do so at his or her own personal peril.

Given under Our Own Hand and
Signed and Sealed
At Our Royal Palace of Pantomime,
VICTORIA

Year of Success 1847.

The sovereign was treated casually while the heir apparent suffered still worse indignities. The fondly cherished notion that there was once, in the good old days of the good old queen, a time when people knew their place and showed due deference to the established authorities surely retreats into the mists of illusion in the face of the "novelty" launched by Messrs Pears in

1888. At the head of an apparently blank sheet of paper was placed the legend

Marvellous Effect
Hold this up to the Light!
England's Hope!

When the fascinated viewer, agog to see what this marvellous effect might be, did hold the leaflet up to the light he revealed a watermarked portrait of Edward Prince of Wales. Suddenly the wording at the bottom of the page took on a new and pungent significance: it read: "Pear's Soap, is England's soap – Prince of soap makers, Soap makers to the Prince." Nor did the soap manufacturers forget Edward when his hopes were realized. At the time of his coronation in 1901 he and his charming, long-suffering queen were recruited to the interests of Maypole Soap. This time the pamphlet in question showed their majesties seated in full regalia on their thrones prepared for the coronation. To witness the Crowning Ceremony the reader was urged to HOLD THIS TO THE LIGHT. This time two crowns sprang into view, on the heads of the King and his Consort.

The Victorians' obsession with hygiene, like the Americans' in our own day, was a standing joke with other nations. The soap makers led the field in the development of English advertising and it was fitting that their endeavours should be sturdily supported by the crown. But it is doubtful whether the Queen did truly realize the importance of soap until the celebration of her Jubilee in 1897. In that year Hudson's, the manufacturers of Lifebuoy, published a little book entitled *The Kings and Queens of England*; each monarch was represented by a portrait captioned with a couple of sentences on the most important events of the reign. For Victoria the rubric runs: "During this reign Hudson's soap was invented."

Of course for a certain section of society the royal family was the focus of interest and their doings, and those of the aristocracy, were matters of supreme importance. In November 1837, the year of Victoria's accession, *Bentley's Miscellany*, edited by "Boz" and illustrated by George Cruikshank, carried an advertisement for "Portraits of the children of the nobility, accompanied by illustrations in verse by distinguished contributors." The series was dedicated to the young Queen. It is hardly surprising that with antecedents like this the Englishman's fascination with the nobility remains as strong as it is today. For their part the upper classes were equally enthralled with the doings of the royal family. In February 1866 Cruickshank himself, now an old man in his seventies, was one of those who received an invitation to view a dessert service made for the Prince of Wales. It was to be seen at 160 New Bond Street and had been made by the firm of Copeland, successors to the company of Josiah Spode. The invitation read: "Mr Copeland, having received permission from H.R.H. the Prince of Wales to exhibit a dessert service recently manufactured for His Royal Highness by his command in Porcelain and Ceramic Statuary, Request the favour of a visit from Mr Cruikshank to inspect the same." Later in the 1890s, Messrs Perry of Regent Street were similarly sending out invitations to a trade showing of a State Dinner Service, also manufactured for the Prince of Wales. The manufacturers were naturally delighted to proclaim these royal commissions while the world at large was eager to see the styles favoured by royalty.

During the reign of Victoria the skills of copywriting in English advertising progressed to become highly specialised. The writers themselves were emerging as a distinct profession by the end of the century and the power of the word was being wielded with increasing sophistication. Yet throughout the period the literary abilities of the ad. man could be completely overwhelmed by a good testimonial for a rival product. No testimonial was higher than the approval of royalty.

9
THE MARKET

"The artificial wants of mankind are becoming more numerous than the natural ones in the present age." The speaker is "Poor Richard" writing in the *Family Almanac* in 1850, his audience the rising middle class of Victorian England. For most Englishmen of that time even the basic natural wants of shelter, food and health were still desperately short, but an increasing number were joining the ranks of a new affluent class, borne up on the shoulders of an industrial process manned by the labouring poor.

The chief result of the Industrial Revolution was to make available to more and more people the way of life and lust for luxury that had previously only been available to the aristocracies of Europe. When the human qualities of mindless greed and wastefulness had been confined to a small minority they had a certain esoteric fascination, but as the nineteenth century advanced into the twentieth and more and more people were able to indulge weaknesses that poverty had denied them, the vicious consequences of mass selfishness gradually became apparent. In our own generation, when the bread of life has taken its place beside the electric tooth brush as but another consumer commodity, and the advanced economies of the world wantonly pillage the resources common to all mankind in the pursuit of an expanding production consumed in frivolous expenditure, to suggest that there is a distinction between man's natural and artificial wants is to invite a charge of naiveté or obscurantism. Yet as we are gradually forced to recognize that the material resources of the planet are finite and will be exhausted in a foreseeable future so we may eventually relinquish the mass production of inessentials and reappraise our priorities.

But here we are looking back into the past, when the monstrous machine of industrialism was still gathering momentum. Then as now its fuel was a mass market and its by-products were frivolous absurdities. In this chapter we shall be looking at some of the characteristics of English Society in the dawn of the consumer age and will glance at some of the artificial wants, easily identified at this distance of time, that we find promoted by the advertisers of the period.

The expanding population, industrialization and increasing affluence provided fertile soil for the growth of manufacturing fortunes in Victorian England. As the market continued to expand the idea that it might become saturated and that demand might flag, could hardly have occurred to a nineteenth century manufacturer in England or America. The state of affairs revealed in the 1950s by Vance Packard's *The Waste Makers* was still in an unforeseeable future. The manufacturer's ideal at least was quality production and consumer durables were intended to be durable. If they were not it was the fault of gimcrack workmanship and not, as today, the result of "planned obsolescence". It was a period when people looked after their possessions and few things were "disposable"; repairs and restoration provided profitable business. The number of advertisements for household dyes is a guide to the temper of the age. People reckoned to wear a garment until it was worn out and, for variety, would dye what they possessed rather than buy something new. Johnson Brothers, a small Birkenhead firm, put the point succinctly in their advertisement which ran: "Why buy a new one?" In the world of planned obsolescence and industrial growth, such a question is heresy but in the 1880s the ancestors of the new consumer class had still not lost the habit of thrift. When they did, decades later, a revolution in public attitudes followed. Victorian consumers, however, were not ready for it.

In one respect, however, they do seem to have been changing. By the end of the century the power of the advertisers was growing apace, and their not always meticulous regard for fair dealing was becoming recognized – in a word, the public was losing its innocence. Thomas Smith, writing in his own press directory in the 1890s, was recommending Ireland as a relatively virgin field for exploitation by his advertiser clients. One of the market's major advantages was, apparently, the decent instincts of the Irish themselves. "The Irish gentry," he wrote, "still retain their simpleness of heart and a consequent belief in the goodness of mankind; hence they answer advertisements very easily." No nineteenth-century advertiser would want to pass up the chance of doing business in a market where people still believed in the goodness of mankind.

Rooted in habits of thrift and rapidly losing his "simpleness of heart", the English consumer might not appear to have been ideal from the advertiser's point of view. But this was only a small part of the story. For the first time in human history a considerable number of people found themselves with the means to indulge in something more than the necessities of life, and the clutter of the Victorian drawing room is a testimony to the eagerness with which the bourgeoisie availed themselves of the chance. The piano was to the Victorians what the motor car is to our own age – a symbol of status, little used, largely unnecessary and in its mass produced form, badly built and designed. And round the shrine formed by the piano clustered that astonishing collection of bric-à-brac despised only a decade ago but now eagerly sought after as though our materialistic age was guiltily anxious to make amends, after years of neglect, to the ghosts of its spiritual ancestors.

While the middle classes steadily amassed the possessions that meant comfort and prestige, others, equally hard working and honest, found their lives collapsing in humiliation and tragedy. In a gardeners' journal published during the early years of the reign we find the following announcement.

> Henry Spare, a well-known Gentleman's Gardener, of known ability and strict integrity, has been a prisoner in Whitecross Street Prison, London, since the 9th of July last for the sum of £28; and he will have to remain in confinement till the middle of January next. The sum is a balance of a debt contracted from 1833 to 1836 for the board and lodging of two of his children who, being in ill health, were sent away for the benefit of a milder climate and their native air. This debt he was unable to discharge from the long and dangerous illness of his wife and the loss of a child who was bed-ridden for fourteen weeks. His wife and children are now in a state of great distress which must increase with the approaching inclement season and he himself is compelled to subsist on the prison allowance as everything belonging to him has been disposed of.

This is something of an extreme case yet, time and time again, when browsing through the Victorian press, one is brought up short by advertisements or news items that clearly come from a different civilization. The most obvious ones are the funny ones, but there are others that raise an eyebrow, not a laugh. What are we to make of the following little tip from "Mrs Riley", in her "Hints to Mistresses of Families" that appeared in the *English Woman's Magazine* for February 1846. She had been stressing the responsibilities that the mistress of a household had for the well-being, both material and moral, of her employees and goes on: "Servants should be paid half yearly and a portion of their wages put into a savings bank. While as to books, those unsuited to a servant's station or prospects should be prohibited."

In our generation the notion of the servant is not dead but we tend to assume, and with reason, that anyone in that mode of employment is there from choice and is, in all respects, beyond the pay packet, a free agent. Today even the wealthiest and most powerful employer who presumes to dictate his servants' reading matter or mode of living is a figure of fun or of contempt. In 1846 such attitudes were normal.

The *English Woman's Magazine* had a middle income readership yet its readers regarded themselves, calmly, as arbiters over the lives of others. Later in the century an advertisement for Calvert's carbolic soap, showing the maid cleaning the floor while the lady of the house stands by, book in hand, observing the effects of the marvellous product, remind us again that the domestic servant was an accepted feature of the middle class household.

The socio-political purpose of the prohibition on books is clear enough but the recommendation as to payment of servants is equally significant and for our purpose specially relevant. A large section of the population was "in service", many living in and most receiving some part of their wages in kind, which in itself reduced their purchasing power. Even such small wages as they did receive might be only half-yearly, and then sizeable amounts would be deducted and put into savings. It is obvious, therefore, that the potential of the consumer market was not being fully realized. That huge segment of the population which was employed in industry was equally restricted in its spending power; to low wages we must add the widespread use of the truck system, another form of payment in kind. With the level of home demand held down by these kinds of factors the manufacturer naturally turned to exporting. Although the nineteenth-century home market was immensely larger than it had ever been before the demand for everything but the necessities of life was confined to the middle classes.

In this sense then, thanks to repressive social policies and an archaic social structure, the English mass consumer market did not realize its full potential. This fact, as much as the taxes on newspapers and advertising that persisted into the middle of the century, must be considered when seeking reasons for the slow development of English advertising techniques. A shrewd contemporary put the matter correctly, though perhaps with undue simplification, when he ascribed the American ascendancy in the field to the much larger American consumption of patent medicines. The patent medicine firms had massive budgets for advertising and despite the huge operations mounted by first Holloway's and then Beecham's in England the total expenditure of all the American companies in the field was larger and a number of the major American agencies built their fortunes on it. "In England," claimed an anonymous contemporary, with some exaggeration, "the poor cannot afford these medicines while the rich, on the slightest hint of ill health, go to a physician."

The omnicompetence of these patent medicines is a constant source of astonishment to a later generation. The Sarsaparilla of Dr J. C. Ayer & Co. of Lowell, Mass., was guaranteed to "dislodge and expel any lurking taint of Scrofula from the system"; the use of Mother Seigel's Curative Syrup would make your head "sit on your shoulders like a flower upon its stalk"; and, most valuable of all, was Blackham's Vegetable Tonic which could utterly destroy the "Death Microbe" itself. Credulity helped to sell patent medicine but so also did the facts of life, such as the high doctors' bills and the appalling state of public health and hygiene.

With good reason the Europeans of the Victorian age doubted the safety of their cities and their water supplies; few who could afford to do otherwise would have drunk from the public water system and consequently the bottling and distribution of natural spa and mineral waters was big business in England as well as on the continent. But the English manufacturer suffered from foreign competition then as now and the waters from the fashionable spas of Germany flooded the English market. A *Special Circular on Imported Natural Mineral Waters*, sent out to their customers by May, Davies and Co., shows that the sluggishness of the English economy was being gloomily detected a century ago. In it the manufacturers urged the superiority of the English over the continental product but they also issued a warning. "Our continental neighbours, who are only too successful in taking the trade out of our hands in so many branches of commerce and manufacture, are threatening us here also."

While May, Davies & Co. preached the virtues of English spa waters the cider industry hoped to boost sales by stressing the medicinal properties of their product and the soft drinks manufacturers also used this argument in their publicity material. Their main support, however, tended to come from the temperance movement. A large sector of the population owed allegiance to the non-conformist churches where the movement was strong and there was a temperance society affiliated to the Church of England. Behind this, no doubt, lay a certain amount of kill-joy Puritanism and priggish self-righteousness; but we should also remember the dimensions of the problem. For the dangers of alcohol to society in the nineteenth century seemed every bit as threatening as those of the addictive drugs of today. The worst excesses of the eighteenth-century gin shops were in the past but the alcohol consumption among all classes of society was a legitimate cause for concern amongst social reformers while its drain on the scanty resources of the industrial poor, looking for some release from the monotony and frequent squalor of their lives, was considerable and disruptive. During the nineteenth century a multitude of temperance drinks were invented which formed the basis of the modern soft drinks industry. They seem to have been popular enough and some, such as Dandelion and Burdock, particularly popular in the north of England, are with us still. Among those which have since faded from the scene were Botanic Beers, made by Masons, who were also the manufacturers of an extract of herbs. This, a kind of do-it-yourself non-alcoholic-drink kit, was, they claimed, the source of the "finest temperance beverage in the world". Despite his address in Wine Office Court, their agent Thomas Smith was himself a total abstainer and we can imagine the enthusiasm with which he attended to this particular account. One of its many rivals, "Orange Champagne", described as the "Drink of the Future", got something of a rave notice in the *Church Times*. The enthusiastic clergyman described it as: "A most delicious non-alcoholic drink, it has all the fizz and go of Moet or Dry Monopole, without the disagreeable after consequences, and for flavour it leaves little to be desired. To all intents and purposes it is a non-intoxicating champagne and by many degrees the nicest drink of its kind."

The reverend reviewer, taking good care to let his readers know that he, at least, was fully *au fait* with the delights of the genuine article, could have learnt something to his advantage from *The Times* offices about drinks without disagreeable after effects. They had found just the thing, a bona fide wine with the required quality, and they gave it a most flattering write up. "There is no wine with which we are acquainted that at all rivals old St Elie in its power of producing exhilaration without disagreeable after consequences." And then, to indicate more specifically the uses to which this excellent beverage could be put, they went on "it is incomparable in refreshing and sustaining those who work with their brains while the rest of the world is sleeping". Clearly the reviewer, together no doubt with the entire editorial office, had been favourably impressed with the sample crate sent for their approval.

With a write up like this the consumer knew more or less where he stood and, indeed, in the wine trade copywriters lapsed into astonishing moments of frankness.

Perhaps the wine merchants themselves wrote the piece, perhaps they were conscious of appealing to a market of connoisseurs, but whatever the reason it is doubtful whether the following would have got past a modern advertising manager, even on the pretext of the softest of the soft sells. "Since 1878, when the phyloxera made its appearance, we have not been able to offer so good value." An advertiser admitting that his product had declined in quality was freakish even in the nineteenth-century; only rarely could the consumer hope for this kind of concession; for the most part he had to look to his own protection.

Throughout our period the claims of the patent medicine-monger, harmless, mendacious or absurd, continued unabated, urging on the public self-styled panaceas that were at best placebos and at worst positively dangerous. In the *laissez faire* atmosphere of the nineteenth-century market the idea of protection in any field was utterly unthinkable. The motto *caveat emptor* "let the buyer beware" was the rule. And usually the best the buyer could hope for in the way of guidance was the disingenuous warnings of rival manufacturers on the malpractices of their competitors.

Occasionally something more serious was attempted, as in 1851 when a certain Mr Wakely published "at the *Lancet* office" a pamphlet entitled *Coffee and its Adulteration.* His findings were given a full report in the *Family Economist* and the net result may be classed as one of the earlier exercises in consumer research. The nub of the article was Mr Wakely's analytical list of the various types of coffee on the market; a few examples will give the gist of his criticisms. "Delicious Coffee" consisted of a mixture of roasted beans and one-third chicory and this was one of the quality brands under review; "Coffee as in France" appears to have been chicory pure and unadulterated. In between the two extremes came a bewildering selection – "Splendid Turkish Coffee", compounded of coffee and chicory in equal quantities; "Fine Plantation Coffee", was two parts of roasted corn to one part chicory. "Parisian Coffee", "Rich Drinking Coffee" and "Fine Java Coffee" were other varieties available. All were undoubtedly nutritious, to judge from the quantities of corn and potatoes that went into their manufacture, but not, it was argued by Mr Wakely, coffee. The trade, feeling obliged to make some reply, waxed indignant. They were not to blame, since they had now been serving chicory so long that the public actually preferred it to coffee and indeed demanded it. The editor of the *Family Economist* was not entirely satisfied. If this was to be the only reaction to proof that the public had for years been "accustomed to drink all sorts of trash as coffee" he could see no reason why other trades should not follow the coffee merchants' example. "Must we now expect," he asked, "that the sausage makers will boldly *proclaim* that they use cats' meat or that the dairies will publicly boast of diluting their milk with horsebrains, chalk and water."

Things did not go quite that far: the proprieties were maintained, at least in public. But unadulterated food seems to have remained something of a luxury. Thirty years after the *Family Economist*'s broadside South Down Farm, Wimbledon decided to distribute a private circular "to our own Customers only" on the subject of cheap adulterated milk. "Knowing that milk is being sold in Wimbledon and Merton at less than the actual cost of production and distribution, we have had samples taken from the carts and barrows of some low price Dairymen, just as the Milk was being delivered to the public, and were not at all surprised to find that it was heavily adulterated with water. It may appear unfair to our fellow tradesmen to inform our Customers of this, although we mention no names, but in self defence and in the interests of the public such practices ought to be exposed."

At least, the people of Merton and Wimbledon could congratulate themselves that the analyst's report commissioned by South Down Farm revealed no horse brains or chalk, but whether the dairy increased its sales as a result of this outspoken exercise in "knocking copy" is not known. It does show, however, that the manufacturer did not have things his own way all the time. In some instances, indeed, he was positively anxious to have his good faith put to the test. In the 1860s the American drive into the English sewing machine market gave rise to a heated rivalry between American and British firms and amongst the Americans themselves. Quite apart from questions of quality the main point at issue was the type of stitch used and the "stitch war" in which the contestants advocated the rival virtues of the lock stitch, the simple stitch and many others engrossed the manufacturers to the exclusion of all else. The housewife was deluged with technical information and analyses, diagrams and testimonials, until, finally, the firm of Wilcox Gibbs took things to their logical conclusion and offered a month's free trial in the home. What has now become common practice with all types of consumer durable was a novelty in the 1860s and seemed to offer the most conclusive testimony to the manufacturers' reliability.

Tests by some third party such as Mr Wakely's analysis of coffees were equally unusual. But in February 1888 an even more rigorous test was run by *The Field* on Scafe's Patent Leather and Rubber Combination Boots. Whether *The Field* had a regular Boot Correspondent is not revealed; if so his job was undoubtedly more taxing than that of his modern equivalent on a motoring magazine. *The Field* subjected the boots to what it called "severe tests" which for rigour might stand comparison with the work of a modern Consumer Association. "A journey of over 100 miles on gravel roads made no appreciable impression on the soles and after 12 hours in the wet grass the feet were as dry and comfortable as possible."

Even as Messrs Scafe launched their remarkable boot the first steps in the transport revolution had already been taken. In 1885 Karl Benz conducted the first road trials of a vehicle driven by an internal combustion engine and before the turn of the century this new form of transport was already making its presence felt. In the late nineties a firm of motor manufacturers, advertising their machines in a Surrey paper, claimed: "It is no optical illusion, our motors will climb the steepest hills in the district at a speed of sixteen miles an hour. We repeat, this is no idle statement but the sworn evidence of a police constable." Few manufacturers could hope for the testimony of the local constabulary in support of their claims but the idea of some form of testimonial was rooted in Victorian advertising philosophy.

In the early 1800s the makers of Watkin's Wonderful Specific Liquid for destroying "that troublesome and loathsome scourge the Black Beetle, which is well known to infest most of the houses in the metropolis", promised as an earnest of their good faith that "four thousand four hundred were destroyed recently in a respectable house in one night, at which any enquirer may be satisfied". One would like to know what etiquette prescribed as the correct reception to be accorded to an enquirer into the number of black beetles recently killed on the premises. This kind of direct testimony was even then unusual and as the century progressed householders became markedly more reticent. But if they were no longer willing to open their doors for the satisfaction of enquirers they still had need of patent carbolic disinfectants for the destruction of house insects and wrote their praises in glowing letters. Such testimonials were most common in the field of patent medicines where they formed an important part of the copywriter's armoury. This is discussed in somewhat fuller detail in the chapter on the Arts of the Copywriter, but of course these letters tell us a good deal about the kind of society they appealed to.

While the poorer had to content themselves with pills and lotions the well-to-do had far more elaborate curatives at their disposal. Some of these, like the numerous electric appliances on the market, were designed to cure the complaints, such as curvature of the spine, thought to be peculiarly the afflictions of the "gentler sections" of society.

The fashion for "electrical treatments" had a long run and they were still being enthusiastically promoted at the end of the century. In 1884 A. Copson Garret, medical electrician of 16 Finsbury Square, was advertising his system of Odo Magnetism in the *English Woman's Year Book* though by this time there were more advanced and convenient systems available as befitted a scientific age. Chief among these were the electric corsets made by Harness or Pulvermacher, which spared the patient the trouble of visiting his doctor and could be worn without "unsightly protuberances" as an everyday garment. Year after year during the closing decades of the century, ladies and gents in a state of becoming undress parade the advertisement pages showing off the full effect of these miraculous contrivances. Like every other patent cure they had their enthusiastic band of devotees. Reasts Patent Invigorator Corsets, for example, which claimed simply to "insure the health" were of course recommended by doctors. But far more telling, with many socially conscious readers, was the fact that the manufacturers were able to produce a letter from the wife of Tankerville Chamberlaine Bey, writing from Cairo.

In the quest for testimonials the makers of Dr Lowder's battery, another of the numerous electrical treatments available, ransacked the past when the present did not offer anything sufficiently impressive. Displaying a nice sense of the occasional ambiguities of the English language they inserted the following notice in Cassell's journal, *Celebrities of This Century*, published in the 1870s. "The Rev. John Wesley, the founder of Methodism, says 'Electricity cures an abundance of diseases, even the most stubborn, many of them in moments, most in a few days, so that it is not only one of the greatest curiosities of the world but one of the noblest boons God ever gave to man.' "

John Wesley had died a century before this "testimonial" of his was published, but he had at least written it. When the mounting demand for testimonials began to outstrip the supply advertisers had to look to alternative sources. One old canvasser readily confessed that "although an honest man" he wrote several testimonials "which were of course, why should I mince the matter, forged". If not written by the advertiser himself testimonials could be bought at a modest price, the clergy being particularly venal in this respect. In America a firm even ran a flourishing business writing testimonials to order and it seems to have been possible to produce enthusiastic witnesses to almost any product.

There was no way of framing legislation that could prevent editors accepting what were known in the trade as "objectionable" advertisements. There were too many allusive ways of wording advertisements for such things as birth control medicines and devices for any statute law to be effective; but right at the end of the century a decision by Mr Registrar Wild in the City of London may have gone some way to stem the tide. The *Weekly Dispatch* had claimed £4 10*s* from an advertising agent in payment for insertions promoting such a product, but the defence made the sly counter-claim that since the advertisement in question had recommended practices that were illegal, the contract was null and void and the plaintiffs could not recover. The judge accepted this line of argument, concurred heartily and argued that since the advertisement was obviously "filthy" the plaintiffs should not have accepted it in the first place. He ruled that the contract was unenforceable.

In those days Britain liked to think of herself as the universal policeman, only unleashing the terrors of her military might in the cause of justice; just like the world powers today she was led to fabricate strange and shaky justifications for wars that were, in reality, fought to advance her imperial and commercial interests. But in general those interests were best served by peace and by opening up the whole world as a market for British goods. The advertising agent came to play an increasing part in the expansion of foreign trade and occasionally agents liked to flatter themselves with the contemplation of their role in the historic imperial mission.

"One of the most interesting chapters in the history of the 19th century, when it comes to be written, will be that describing the services of advertising agents as empire builders. Commerce even more than sentiment binds the ocean sundered portions of the Empire together. Anyone who increases these commercial interests strengthens the whole fabric of the empire . . . while if there is trouble, say in the Far East, the advertising agent is one of the first to feel the results of the uneasiness and anxiety." So wrote one editor, while the manager of T. B. Browne's exclaimed on one occasion: "We are the real members of the Peace Society."

The point is pressed home by the advertisers' reactions to news of British successes in opening up new markets abroad. In November 1858 news came through that British troops had triumphed once again over the antiquated armaments of the Imperial Chinese Army – they were even able to burn the imperial summer palace at Pekin before the Treaty of Tien Tsin guaranteed British opium traders free access to a number of ports. But the opium trade was not the only one to benefit. Strachan and Co., Dealers in Fine Tea of 28 Cornhill opposite the Royal Exchange, took space in the advertisement pages of the *Family Friend* to make an announcement to tea drinkers. This said that the war with China was over, that open communication with China was now a "fact beyond recall" and that as a result tea prices must inevitably fall – none more so than the price of Strachan's tea.

British traders were affected by other people's wars too. During the American Civil War British cotton prices were affected because the Lancashire mill workers refused to work cotton which came from the slave plantations of the Southern States. To our generation, mesmerized by the "If-we-don't-some-one-else-will" argument regarding sanctions, such loyalty to principle is bound to seem somewhat quaint; to the workers themselves it meant the loss of the jobs they badly needed; to the shopkeeper it meant a rise in prices. Among the tradesmen of Islington for example H. & C. Glave and C. R. Carpenter were directly affected. Each no doubt egged on by the example of the other they both announced that their prices would remain unaltered despite the "recent advance in price caused by the Civil War in America".

The Boer war involved a much larger section of the British public and advertisers were not slow to cash in on the patriotic fervour generated by the first real war England had had for more than a generation. Although Britain achieved her military victory it had been touch and go and at home the advertisers had done their bit to boost public morale. In the light of one of Lord Roberts' dispatches from the front, the makers of Monkey Brand soap could not resist a pun. The dispatch read: "French is scouring the country." A picture shows General French in his tent, a map spread out before him, with the Monkey Brand monkey at his elbow offering a bar of the famous soap and promising that this "will scour the country". What better munition could be found, suggests the caption, for scouring? Such ready wit failed the copywriter engaged by Messrs Wallace, Bailey and Wilkins, manufacturers of a New Strap Legging for the troops at the front, made of REAL PIG SKIN. The market for strap leggings no doubt comprised stern practical men who were more words of L. C. R. Duncombe Jewell, Special War Correspondent of the *Morning Post* with the third Division S.A. Field Forces 1899–1900 that carried weight. "The Dennison Legging", he wrote, "decidedly surpasses the expectation of its merits which your advertisements led me to form; and I have no hesitation in pronouncing it to be quite the best strap legging now in the field."

Manufacturers of less functional products had to look for more alluring means of persuasion. The makers of Sen-Sen, a throat ease and breath perfume, devised the Sen-Sen War Game, with which to hold their readers' interest. The board consisted of a ring marked off in segments to represent Pretoria, Johannesburg, Bloemfontein, Natal and three other prison camps. The pieces had to be moved so that the Union Jack covered Pretoria and British troops occupied the other territories, while the Boers were safely neutralized in the camps. The game, which would have not overtaxed the most low witted sufferer from halitosis, was noticeably less difficult than the version played out by General Roberts. Nevertheless in 1900 he returned to England thinking that he had won, only to find that a series of Boer victories proved him mistaken, and French and Kitchener had to be sent out to make victory a reality. They forced the Boers to a treaty and in doing so conducted a campaign which, by chance one assumes rather than by design, spelt out the word Bovril across the long suffering lands of southern Africa. The writing was hardly copperplate but routes on the map required only a minimum of ingenuity to bring out the meat of the message.

The domestic market was the most important one for many Victorian advertisers and they angled their appeal to the ladies of the household in what today seems a rather quaint way.

It has long been accepted that the Victorians were prudes where sex was concerned. The topic was apparently never discussed in polite society and this inhibition is assumed to have extended to every class. Urged on perhaps by the wish to find antecedents of contemporary attitudes and in the conviction that the Victorians, since they were human, must have been interested in this most human of all concerns, recent writers have been cheerfully turning up evidence to correct the earlier stereotype. Some of the finest collections of pornography were assembled under the aegis of the unwitting Queen, and prostitution was so generally widespread that it was hardly worth noting even by those whose notions of propriety allowed them to discuss such things. Yet early sociological surveys brought up facts and figures that might shock even our own "permissive" ears while many a staid paterfamilias expected his daughter's prospective husband to have had enough experience to guarantee her a satisfactory wedding night. Nobody bothered to question too closely where such experience was to come from.

No doubt the goings on of high society shocked the middle class household and no doubt the rites of the marriage bed were less openly discussed than now. But the Victorians were neither complete fools nor complete hypocrites and the advertisement pages in women's and family magazines of the period show that hygienic and cosmetic devices were used as much as today.

An article on menstruation and the status of women in Victorian society (in the modern journal *Victorian Studies* (1970)) is both an interesting and depressing investigation of social attitudes. It shows the uphill struggle of the more enlightened publicists to break down the taboos that surrounded the whole subject and the way in which obscurantist polemicists used the fact of the monthly period as an argument for the natural inferiority of women to men. But if the subject was thought unfit for intelligent public debate outside the learned journals there was at least one area of publication where it was freely mentioned. The hygenic sanitary towel was an important invention of Victorian times and the manufacturers and advertisers of this article had no interest in or time for the pseudo-scientific or popular sort of debate. Neither did they have any inhibitions in promoting their valuable product.

After their introduction in the 1870s there were regular advertisements for Southalls Sanitary Towels in such respectable journals as *Cassels Family Magazine* and the *English Illustrated Magazine*. In the *English Woman's Year Book* an advertisement takes the form of an announcement in heavy Gothic script against a background of meshed black lines. "Eminent medical authorities" regularly endorsed them as admirable inventions for women's comfort while Miss A. Cooper, a nurse, tells how she has recommended them to patients and friends, all of whom had been delighted.

Still more familiar to the modern eye are the advertisements for corsetry. In April 1885 Messrs Hovens were able to proclaim proudly that the garter had been entirely superseded by the stocking suspender, and backed up their claim with an illustration. The ladies in the picture are undoubtedly members of the "polite world" – the same polite world which approved of Thomson's glove fitting corset. Victorian family and women's magazines are littered with illustrations of those mighty structures that contained and restrained the buxom figures of our ancestors.

But there were those with another problem: for them the advertisements could offer the Thin Bust "Ideal" or the Health Braided Wire Dress Form. Both would ensure that "vulgar" and (far worse) "instantly detected pads would be discarded forever." The latter, produced by the American Wire Braided Company, was also hygienic and (god save the mark) "recommended by physicians to every Lady who uses artificial means to promote symmetry of form". Thousands, the reader is assured, are already wearing them with secret delight but, a nice psychological touch, "If you can't obtain them from your draper and he REFUSES to order them for you, send a postal order." No one need suffer the embarrassment of actually going to a shop and asking for the things while the thoughtful manufacturer provides the final safeguard of modesty: "All parcels are sent by post; are entirely secured from observation; nothing whatever on outside of package to denote its contents." Perhaps such public notices of the frailties of the fair sex shocked some Victorian ladies by their frankness. In our own decade, on the other hand, women have shown their disgust with the whole inhibiting notion of the brassière by forming organizations to boycott it. Modern Women's Lib. is also bitterly conscious of the traitors within – those giddy-headed quislings who collaborate with the male enemy by wearing fashionable clothes and buying fashionable magazines.

The Victorian girl had her fashion "glossies" too. These took themselves seriously and were as liable to scathing comments from the philistine public as their modern contemporaries. *Le Folet*, one of the plushiest of them all, found itself involved in a running battle with *Punch* after an extremely bad translation of a French article on fashion had provoked a delighted bellow from the latter. In December 1864 the editor of *Le Folet* returned the attack in "A Word with Punch". "Our word with our deformed contemporary, whose mind in this instance appears as much warped as his body, is to complain of a recent miserable attempt, in an article headed *Flowers from Le Folet*, to fasten upon a word in our translated article on fashion an offensive meaning and one which none but a gross mind would for a moment think of attaching to it." For the readers of *Le Folet* maintaining their dignity was a full time occupation; it was threatened even in the commonplace hazards of daily living without the editor of *Punch* adding to the difficulties. However, thanks to their editor, he had been put in his place and now, thanks to the promises of E. Philpott, family draper and Jupon manufacturer, it looked as though ladies were to be spared other embarrassments hitherto all too common.

Mr Philpott, having recently perfected the Sansflectum Ondina Crinoline, hastened to bring his invention to the attention of the public. As well as being a benefactor he seems also to have been a model advertiser for he offered a pamphlet – a practice considered *de rigeur* by all the best agents. In this instance the enquirer would have received an illustrated booklet on the History of Crinolines from 1559 to 1863, written by one of those gentlemen of proved literary talent who peopled the office of the Victorian advertising agent. And Philpott must have used an agent. He had, after all, produced a new discovery sufficiently important to demand the attention of journalists and had need of someone able to "find means to induce an editor to create an interest by a special notice".

Who that agent was we do not know but the editor was he of the *Ladies Newspaper*. His words were quoted avidly and to powerful effect in Philpott's advertisements:

> The patent Ondina or Waved Jupon does away with the unsightly results of ordinary hoops and so perfect are the wave-like bands that a lady may ascend a steep stair, lean against a table, throw herself into an arm chair, pass her stall at the opera, or occupy a fourth seat in a carriage without inconvenience to herself or others, or provoking the rude remarks of the observers – thus modifying in an important degree all those peculiarities tending to destroy the modesty of English women.

A gel certainly had to run the gauntlet in the good old days.

Mr Steitz, who advertised in the *English Illustrated Magazine*, had a very practical approach to balls, theatres and concerts. Satisfied that a young lady could at least be trusted to choose a ballroom dress he had turned his attention to the mechanical aspects of the matter and had come up with his own, patented, fan and programme holder. This had the immense advantage of rendering fan girdles unnecessary. These had formerly been worn round the waist, with often detrimental effects on the figure, but the new fan and programme holder could be attached to *any* part of the dress and shortened while dancing. This could be especially useful at fancy dress balls when guests tended to be laden down with papier mâché sceptres and so forth.

In the ballroom or at the dinner party the Victorian women enjoyed some compensation for the subordinate role she was obliged to play in most other social environments. Here convention entitled her to deference and consideration. It was of course a carefully restricted privilege and this game of chivalry was recognized as a charade by both the parties to it. In the home, however, married women did exercise considerable authority and controlled the housekeeping. For women of the middle classes and above this was not so paltry a thing as it would seem today. In a period when any moderately well-off household would employ a couple of servants and a wealthy house might employ a staff of a dozen or more, the title of Mistress of the House was not an empty one. The members of her family and the servants often added up to a sizeable little community whom the wife was responsible for feeding, clothing and so on. A husband might well delegate the power of hiring and firing to his wife who would also have to keep the home budget in balance and see that money was spent well at the shops. Like the manager of a small hotel she would be faced with problems of petty pilfering and staff discipline and, in that ostentatiously moralistic age, was held by some to be responsible for the spiritual well being and the good behaviour of her servants. The job was limited and confining yet within those limits it demanded considerable organizational ability and the exercise of responsibility. It may not be entirely fortuitous that the origins of the suffragettes, the first "Women's Lib", are to be found in the decades when social change was beginning to reduce the numbers of people in domestic service rapidly and extensively and the responsibilities of the bourgeois ladies who launched the movements of protest were being correspondingly reduced.

In the home, at least, the Victorian wife, while always the junior partner, had an important and interesting share in running the "family firm". But in the world at large she was prevented, at every turn, from living the same sort of independent and mobile life that a man assumed was his birthright. Even to meet socially could present problems to a woman if she wished to do so in a public place. Beyond visiting at certain well established times of the day a woman could not meet with her friends freely. The natural haunts of men were barred to women while many of the restaurants and cafés were not considered fit places for ladies to visit unless attended by male escorts.

The Holborn Restaurant, 218 High Holborn, was, its proprietors confidently believed, one of the sights and one of the Comforts of London. And well it might have been, for it offered "the attraction of the chief Parisian establishments with the quiet and order essential to English customs". What more could one ask for than to sit down to its famous table d'hôte dinner to the accompaniment of "high class instrumental music of a refined character, directed by an eminent conductor". But during the daytime this excellent establishment took on another character and served another function, as the advertiser indicates. "Ladies attending Exhibitions or out shopping will find at the Holborn Restaurant quiet, attention and comfort." The following year the first of the ABC tea shops were opened; and as their numbers increased it was soon generally accepted that ladies could pass the time of day together unchaperoned in public. Up till this decade opportunities for such meetings were rare and restaurants like the Holborn few and far between.

It is the view of Roger Fulford in his book, *Votes for Women*, that the tea shop of the 1880s and 1890s, where women could easily meet friends of their own choice rather than acquaintances dictated by their husbands, was one of the basic causes behind the burgeoning power of the suffragettes. And these places must have served to spread ideas and recruit commitment to a common cause. But for more than a decade before the first ABC restaurant opened its doors, journals like the *English Woman's Review* were demonstrating the practical implications of demands for women's equality. Each monthly number dealt with current political and economic problems and often the only thing to betray that the magazine was for women as such was the title.

Even the highly intelligent and determined blue stockings of the suffragette movement shared the weaknesses of the age for patent medicine – Samuel Barlow, Chemist of Darlington, thought it worth his while to advertise Barlow's powders, guaranteed to "cure Tic-Doloreux, or Pains in the teeth, face, head etc." But any Victorian advertising manager would expect to fill their pages and budget with this kind of thing. More germane to the purpose of the *English Woman's Review* was the following which appeared in the number for October 1868.

> Belgravia Photographic Company and
> Ladies' School of Photography
> Under the Patronage of the Society for the Promoting of the Employment of Women.
> The manager will make every endeavour to ensure excellence in the work done, so as to challenge comparison with the best houses, while the scale of charges will be extremely moderate.

The aims of the journal and the aims of the society indicate the growing power of the movement for women's equality. But the tone of the advertisement firmly roots it in its period. The whole thing is infected by the feeling of a school girl on probation, and no wonder: all the officers of the Society were men.

The fight for women's rights was to be a long one and in the early years even the most positive campaign seemed to evaporate in the fog of public opinion. Mrs Millicent Garrett Fawcett one of the pioneers of women's rights who hoped to win the day by argument rather than militancy, had the sword turn in her hand as she attempted to cut a way through the cushioning layers of public complacency. In the early days the majority of women were their own worst enemies, agreeing with men that the sexes had their allotted places and that women had best keep to theirs; but rarely was the case put with such bland obtuseness as in this advertisement by the makers of RIZINE, ask-your-grocer-for-it, baking powder.

Rizine's sponsors seemed ready to concede women's rights without a fight; for this was in the days when the customer was always right. Entitled *The Excellence of Women* the advertisement crooned "We have had many proofs of women's excellence. Mrs Fawcett and others have shown beyond doubt that women are the intellectual equals of men, if not their superiors. So long as they do not merge the woman into the scholar all is well, but women's province is to charm to edify to minister . . . and nowhere are a woman's attributes more noticeable than in the kitchen where with dainty fingers and skilful brain she busies herself preparing pleasant surprises for her husband and her children. For to 'ring the changes' on standard foods is the delight of her life." Poor Mrs Fawcett: surely she didn't mean quite that. Well possibly not, but if she and the rest of England's women were going to stop "busying" themselves in this way, who, for goodness sake, was going to sell them an ounce of RIZINE? And so it happened that the anonymous copywriter worked his way in one easy paragraph from a plea for women's rights to a hard sell for baking powder.

But in at least one surprising respect the sexes were more "equal" in Victoria's England than they are today. Palmerston, Prime Minister from 1855 to 1858 and again from 1859 to 1865, is thought to have been the last British statesman to wear make-up and at the beginning of the sixties the Perfumiers Piesse and Lubin of No. 2 New Bond Street were most attentive to his requirements and to all of their male clients. Their price list includes *Prince Arthur's Choice* and *His Royal Highness the Prince of Wales' Perfume* as well as *Her Majesty's Perfume*, *Chinese Bouquet*, etc. Other scents are obviously designed for the girls and the names may have an unexpected ring – *Love Charm*, 1862; *Follow-Me-Lads*, 1862; *Stolen Kisses*, 1861 (further down is listed its "sequel" *Box-his-ears*) and *Kiss me Quick*. What with seduction and "uni-sex" established in the copywriter's repertoire we seem to be in the wrong century.

Modern studies of the Victorians remind us how much our social structure and attitudes derive from the first century of industrialism. We can trace the outlines of the consumer society emerging from at least the 1850s and it is not surprising that advertising, so much the child of that kind of society, should win its independence during the same period.

Before the industrial age, the main obstacle to the spread of the basic comforts of life throughout the social hierarchy was the inadequacy of the production process. Fifty years after the development of successful production techniques, consumption, not production, was beginning to pose problems for the manufacturer. To a later age, one of the more amusing aspects of Victorian life is the proliferation of patent gadgets, from the electropathic body-belt, to the portable home Turkish bath. No doubt our grand-children will find such unnecessary marvels as the plastic sweat suit or the self-stirring pan, equally diverting. But all are symptoms of a common disease caused by the need for manufacturers to create markets which will take up excess productive capacity.

In the 1950s, American market consultants and advertising men were voicing alarm at the possibility that "America's capacity to produce is fast outstripping her capacity to consume". Nineteenth-century England had certainly not reached that bleak plateau of human achievement, but the signs were there. As productivity grew it became increasingly obvious that sales methods had to be improved and that new techniques had to be devised to attract consumers. Of these techniques the most important was advertising, which was revolutionized in the nineteenth century and raised to the rank of a major and increasingly profitable business.

In this book we hope to have shown how Victorian advertisers, while responding to the prejudices and dreams of the Victorian consumers, helped to shape their attitudes. We have also attempted to trace the roots of advertising as an industry and to show how, within a comparatively short time, it came to occupy a major place in the commercial world of Victorian England.

VICTORIAN ADVERTISING IN PICTURES

I THE MEDIA

GREATCENTRALCIGARST
NATIONAL ASSEMBLY ROOMS HIGH HOLBORN
OPEN FOR DANCING
ADMISSION ONE SHILLIN
A & H. ISA
The TRADE
SKINNER IMPORTER
PAPER HANGER

PUBLIC OPINION 2d WEEKLY
CROSBY'S BALSAMIC COUGH ELIXIR
AMERICAN WATCH COMPANY
EVERY DISEASE OF THE EYE CURED BY EDE'S PATENT AMERICAN EYE LIQUID
ALLAN ROYAL MAIL STEAMERS
Canada AND UNITED STATES
COOK'S TOURS
WATCHES & CLOCKS
John Bennett's 64 & 65 CHEAPSIDE
The Echo
Dr ROOKES ANTI-LANCET GRATIS
PIESSE & LUBIN OPOPONAX
The PRO-RATA PRINCIPLE Spiers and Pond
CHEQUE BANK CHEQUES RECEIVED HERE
EMANUEL DIAMOND & PEARL MERCHANT, SILVERSMITH 27, OLD BOND STREET
Mr STREETER 18, NEW BOND St LONDON, W. MANUFACTURER 18 CARAT GOLD GEM JEWELLERY
FELTOE AND SONS, SPECIALITE SHERRY
CONDUIT STREET, LONDON. MANCHESTER & BRIGHTON.
THE GREAT FAMILY MEDICINE OF THE AGE.
KEATINGS COUGH LOZENGES BEST & SAFEST REMEDY. OF ALL CHEMISTS.
GOODALLS QUININE WINE
YORKSHIRE RELISH
CHLORODYNE
LAMPLOUGH'S PYRETIC SALINE, IS PLEASANT & CURES HEADA BILIOUSNESS & SKIN AFFECT
DAILY NEWS
JUDY PRICE 2d WEEKLY
THE PALL MALL GAZETTE.
DAILY TELEGRAPH LARGEST CIRCULATION IN THE WORLD.
BILLIARDS THURSTON & Co
OCEAN, RAILWAY, & GENERAL TRAVELLERS' ASSURANCE COMPANY,
INSURANCE AGAINST ALL KINDS OF ACCIDENTS BY LAND AND SEA.
JOHN BRINSMEAD & SONS GOLD MEDAL PIANOS 18, WIGMORE St LONDON, W.
BURGLAR-PROOF SAFES. FIRE-RESISTING SAFES. CHATWOOD,
120, CANNON STREET, LONDON.
W.H. SMITH & SON 186, STRAND.

1.1 Although it had roots in the past, advertising was undoubtedly a 19th century invention. From the 1830's onwards it dominated much of the environment as it does today

1.2 *Below* Once the tax on newspaper advertisements was abolished in 1855 advertisers could exploit this fruitful medium to the full

1.3 The sandwich board man was a familiar sight in the streets of Victorian London and a favourite butt of cartoonists

"Rather hard lines to have such a cough, and trudge about all day with an advertisement of an infallible remedy on your back, and not a shilling to buy a box with."

1.4 Horse drawn omnibuses quickly became popular advertising outlets

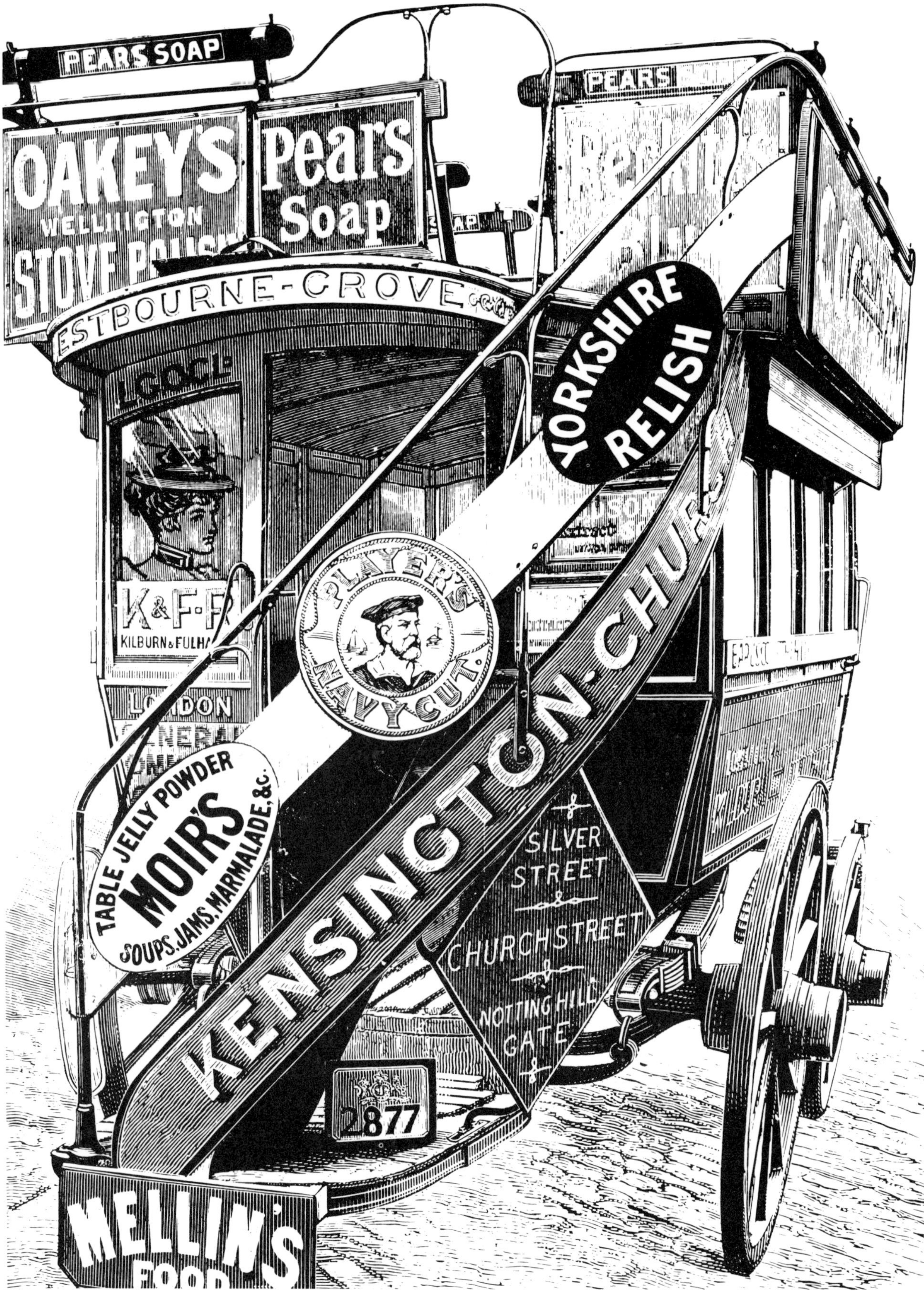

OMNIBUS ADVERTISING CONTRACT.

	No. of Omnibuses.	Routes Marked.
Bank to Elephant and Castle -	- 7	
Barnsbury to Kennington Gate	- 11	
Bayswater (Starch Green) to Liverpool St.	14	
Bayswater (Shepherd's Bush) to L'pool St.	14	
Do. do. do. to Mile End	29	
Blackwall to Piccadilly Circus-	22	
Bow to Charing Cross -	- 19	
Brompton to Bank *via* Victoria Station	- 15	
Brompton to Liverpool St. Stn., G.E.R. -	8	
Do. to London Bridge -	- 9	
Do. to Kilburn *via* Notting Hill	- 21	
Brompton (West) to Holloway	- 18	
Brompton to Islington -	- 24	
Camden Town to Camberwell ("*Waterloo*")	9	
Do. do. to Waterloo Station	- 4	
Camden Town to Victoria Station	- 34	
Camden Town to Kennington Gate	- 12	
Chelsea to Old Ford -	- 12	
Chelsea to Hoxton - -	- 12	
Clapton to Piccadilly Circus -	- 10	
Clapham to Gracechurch Street	- 6	
Cricklewood to Charing Cross	- 8	
Farringdon St. Ry. to Elephant & Castle	6	
Hackney to Bank - -	- 8	
Hackney to Walworth -	- 6	
Hackney to Piccadilly Circus -	- 7	
Hampstead to Piccadilly Circus	- 7	
Hammersmith to Lv'pool St. Stn., G.E.R.	32	
Do. to Caledonian Road *via* Shaftesbury Avenue -	- 15	
Hammersmith to Victoria	- 15	
Harlesden Green to Charing Cross	- 3	
Highbury Corner to Highbury Barn	- 4	
Holloway (Hornsey Rise) V.S. ("*Favorite*")	14	
Holloway (Tollington Park) to Vic. Stn.	14.	

	No of Omnibuses.	Routes Marked.
Holloway (Archway Tavern)	12	
Holloway (Finsbury Park) -	- 12	
Islington to Old Kent Road -	- 20	
Kennington to Charing Cross	- 12	
Kensal Green to London Bridge	- 35	
Kensal Green to Charing Cross	- 10	
Kilburn to Fenchurch Street Station	- 23	
Kilburn to Charing Cross -	- 7	
Kilburn to Victoria Station -	- 7	
Kilburn to Willesden -	- 2	
Kingsland to Elephant and Castle	- 16	
Notting Hill to Liverpool St. Stn., G.E.R. ("*John Bull*") -	- 24	
Oxford Street to Euston Road	- 4	
Old Ford to Bank - -	- 12	
Paddington, Harrow Road (Prince of Wales) to London Bridge	- 6	
Wormwood Scrubbs to Charing Cross	- 18	
Paddington (Royal Oak) to Victoria Stn.	6	
Pimlico (Victoria Station) to Oxford Circus, *via* Bond Street -	- 7	
Pimlico (Victoria Station) to King's Cross Station - -	- 10	
Putney to Liverpool Street -	- 40	
Stoke Newington to Victoria Station	- 20	
St. John's Wood to Lon. B. ("*City Atlas*")	13	
St. John's Wood to Camberwell ("*Atlas*")	21	
Strand to Waterloo Station -	- 4	
Uxbridge Road to Charing Cross	- 8	
Waterloo Station, S.W.R., to King's Cross, G.N.R. -	- 6	
Westminster and Pimlico to Bank	- 8	
West Kilburn and London Bridge	- 11	
West Kilburn and Charing Cross	- 9	
Do. do and Victoria -	- 4	

ease place ......50...... Advertisements 7' 10" × 1' 8" ....

Out side the Omnibuses on the Routes marked on the above List, for which I agree pay the **LONDON GENERAL OMNIBUS COMPANY,** Limited, £4=13=9 per week

.... commencing ~~when all are fixed~~ Aug 9/90, but should any or all of the dvertisements be removed or discontinued by you during the term of this Contract, proportionate allowance shall be made me.

Name R. Brown for W. F. Morrison

Address Covent Garden Theatre

Date August 4th 1890

THOMAS SMITH,

SOLE CONTRACTOR FOR

ADVERTISING ON AND IN THE OMNIBUSES

OF THE

LONDON GENERAL OMNIBUS COMPANY.

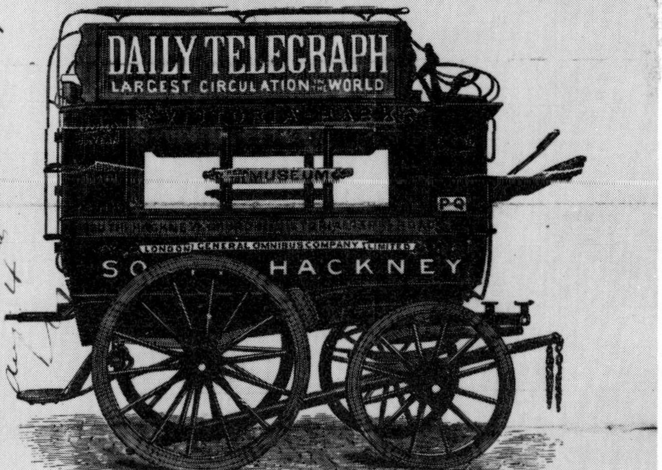

TERMS FOR ADVERTISING:

OUTSIDE THE OMNIBUSES.

SIZE - { 8 FEET BY 20 INCHES. 12/6 PER MONTH, PER PLATE.
6 FEET BY 18 INCHES. 10/- PER MONTH, PER PLATE.

Painting each Advertisement once a year, 20s., twice a year, 30s.

INSIDE THE OMNIBUSES.

1.5 Placing advertisements inside buses caused something of a public outcry at first. By the 1890's such protests were long out of date and the "Crusty old Gentleman" of this cartoon was fighting a losing battle

1.6 In 1896, on the eve of the introduction of motor vehicles onto London Streets, the *Illustrated London News* proposed alternative employment for horses

THE REAL STREET OBSTRUCTIONS.

1.7 From the 1830's the advertising cart had been part of the London street. This cartoon makes a biting comment on the scourge of advertising

1.8 The bill sticker's only concern was to find somewhere to stick his bills; if they covered someone elses so much the better. Bill sticking was a scourge, not only because it papered city streets but, in the view of one cartoonist at least, because of the corrupting message it publicised. Violence in entertainment is not unique to our times

1.9 Towards the end of the century, bill stickers were somewhat better disciplined

1.10 Advertisers became increasingly aware of the importance of site. A new station indicator on the London underground railway gave Bovril a fine position for their advertisements

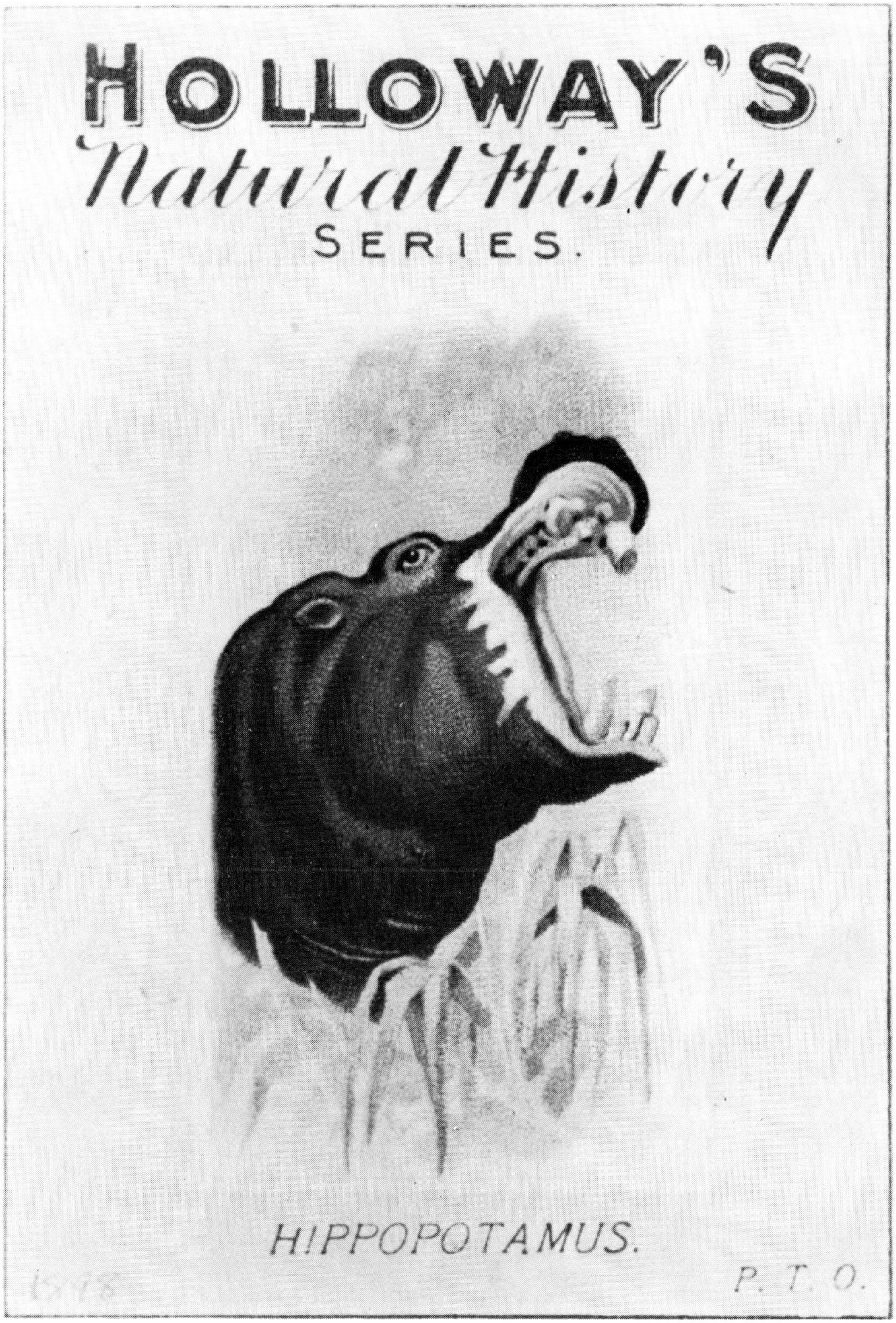

2.1 Illustrated general knowledge cards, monopolized later by cigarette manufacturers, were used by other advertisers in the 19th century

2.2 Victorian retailers fully appreciated the value of the paper bag as a means of promotion. The art of packaging was still in its infancy, but this factory scene comes from a bag of the firm that made it

2.3 Pictorial calendars were a favourite subject for packaging at Christmas time, as this picture of a calendar printed on a paper bag shows

1868

JANUARY

FEBRUARY

MARCH

APRIL

MAY

JUNE

JULY

AUGUST

SEPTEMBER

OCTOBER

NOVEMBER

DECEMBER

JOHN GREAVES,
TEA AND COFFEE MERCHANT,
34, EAST CLAYTON STREET,
NEWCASTLE-ON-TYNE.

T. SHEARD,

GROCER AND TEA DEALER,

21, High-Street, OXFORD.

Hill's Superior Biscuits.---British Wines.

M. Billing, 75 and 76, Newhall-Street, Birmingham.

THE CITY OF CHIN-KIANG-FOO

Is more than four miles in circumference. The parapet being so thick and strong that cannon balls had scarcely any effect on it. The garrison, at the time of the attack, consisted of 3,000 men, of whom 1,000, and 40 Mandarias of rank were killed. The first man who mounted the top of the wall was Lieutenant Cuddy, of the Grenadier Company of the 55th: he behaved with matchless gallantry—slowly, but firmly, he climbed the ladder; on reaching the top he waved his sword, and then assisted his men over; but receiving a wound, whichdisabled him for the rest of the day, he sat down, bound it up, and continued cheering on his men till the close of the attack. The Tartars fought with great bravery—made repeated charges on our men with their long spears, and disputed every inch of ground. The loss of the British, killed and wounded, was—Navy 24, Army 145; total 169.

2.4 Another bag. Current affairs, and particularly the triumphs of British arms, were always good copy

2.5 The well-named Mr. Smart of Wimbledon wrappered his customer's purchases in a picture of his own premises

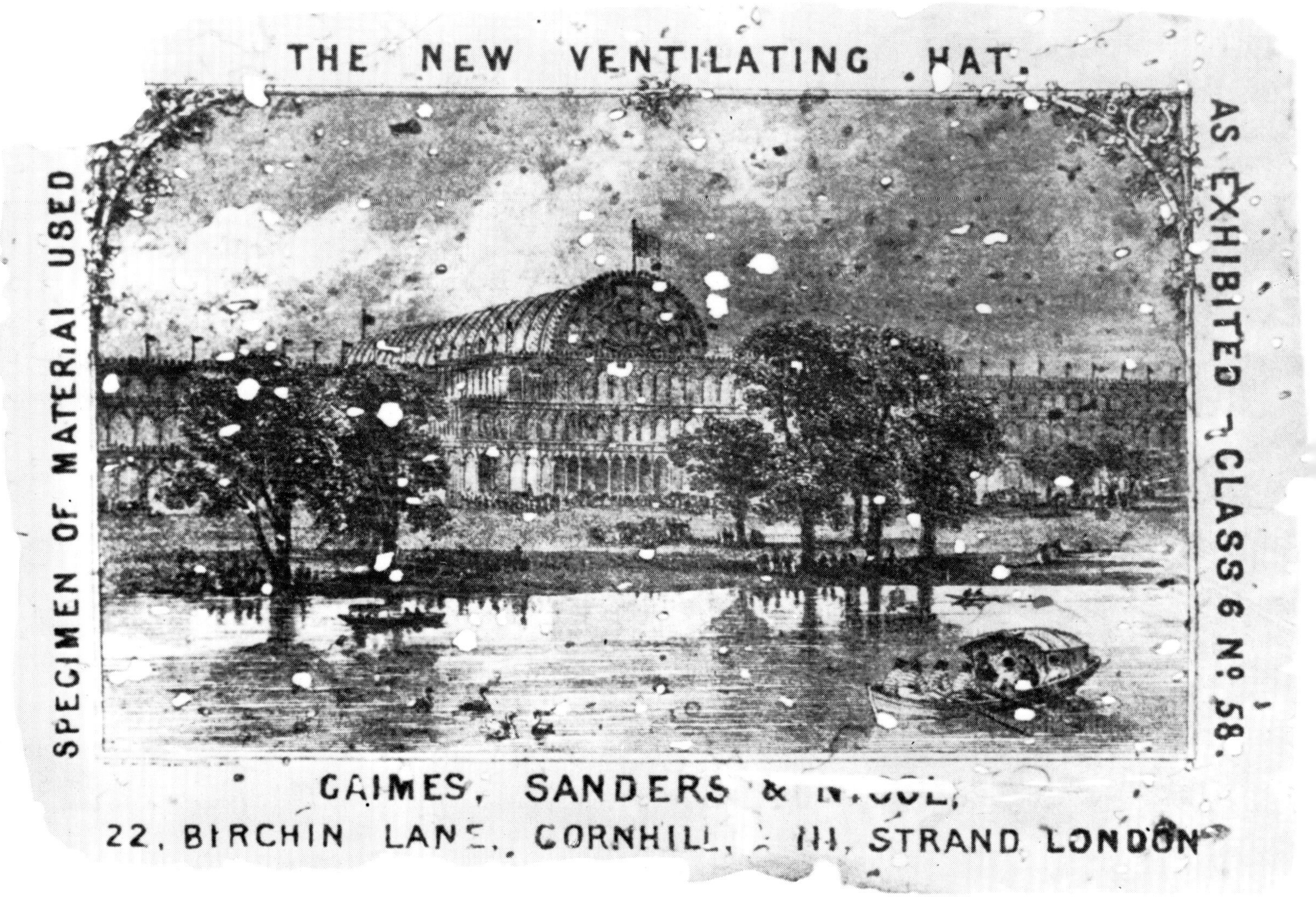

2.6 This picture of the Crystal Palace was printed on the perforated cork used for the ingenious ventilating hat, exhibited at the Great Exhibition of 1851

2.7 To have one's friendly "Good Morning!" answered by "Have you used Pear's soap" became somewhat tedious after a while
2.8 Beechams exploited the Victorian passion for drawing-room ballads by running its own Music Portfolio as a promotion
2.9 A Christmas give-away by Colman's Mustard

MESSRS PEARS OFFER YOU THEIR BOOKMARKER
(Try how it alters your expression)
Good morning!
Have you used
Pears' Soap?

BEECHAM'S
MUSIC
PORTFOLIO
BEECHAM'S
PATENT PILLS
ST. HELENS LANCASHIRE
TRADE MARK
No. 19
REGISTERED.
BANJO PRAISES.
COPYRIGHT EDITION.
PRESENTED BY
A WONDERFUL MEDICINE.
CANNING & CO., LITH 3, RIDGMOUNT ST. W.C

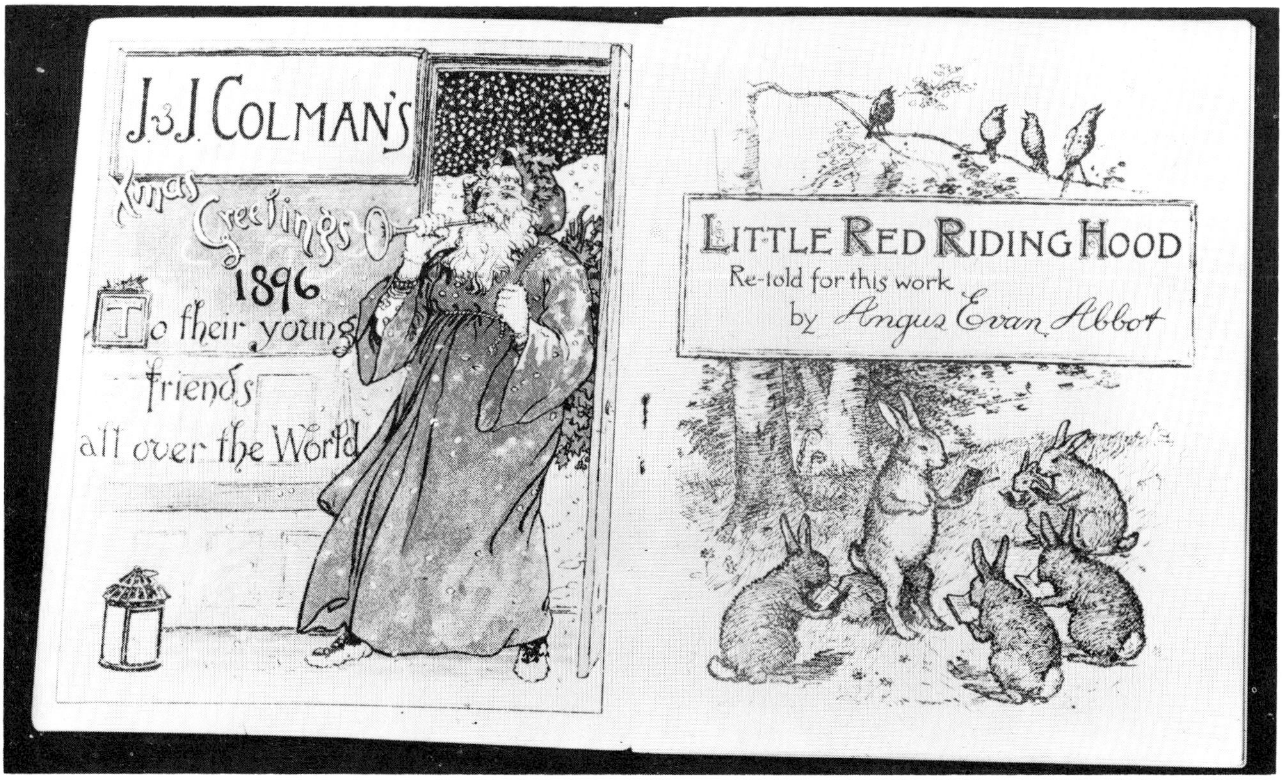
J. & J. COLMAN'S
Xmas
Greetings
1896
To their young
friends
all over the World
LITTLE RED RIDING HOOD
Re-told for this work
by Angus Evan Abbot

Thu.	1	Empress of India, 1877
Fri.	2	**"Ruby" Matches, 1862**
Sat.	3	"Mooltan," 1849
Sun.	4	**Tinder-box with its "fyr-**
Mon.	5	**stan" known to Saxons**
Tue.	6	Dividends due on Consols
Wed.	7	**Pillar Post Wax Vestas, '78**
Thu.	8	**Bryant & May's Luminous**
Fri.	9	**Box-holder, 1879**
Sat.	10	Royal Exchange burnt, 1838
Sun.	11	**"Congreve" Matches,**
Mon.	12	**50 for 2 6, 1830**
Tue.	13	St. Hilary
Wed.	14	Battle of Rivoli, 1797
Thu.	15	**"Tiger" Matches, 1864**
Fri.	16	"Corunna," 1809
Sat.	17	"Falkirk, 1746
Sun.	18	German Empire procl'd, '71
Mon.	19	"Ciudad Rodrigo," 1812
Tue.	20	London Docks opened, 1799
Wed.	21	Louis XVI. beheaded, 1793
Thu.	22	"Rorke's Drift," 1879
Fri.	23	William Pitt died, 1806
Sat.	24	**"Nigger" Wax Mat'es, '87**
Sun.	25	Conversion of St. Paul
Mon.	26	"Khartoum," 1885
Tue.	27	**"Eupyrion" Match inv. '05**
Wed.	28	"Aliwal," 1846
Thu.	29	First Reformed Parliam't, '33
Fri.	30	Charles I. beheaded, 1649
Sat.	31	Surrey Theatre burnt, 1865

Wed.	1	Bismarck b., 1815
Thu.	2	Cobden d., 1865
Fri.	3	"Quebec" fd. by the French [1608
Sat.	4	St. Ambrose
Sun.	5	Oliver Goldsmith d., 1774
Mon.	6	Old Lady Day
Tue.	7	**"Turtle" Match Stand, '86**
Wed.	8	King of Denmark b., 1818
Thu.	9	Lord Bacon d., 1626
Fri.	10	**B. & M.'s Wax Matches ofd.**
Sat.	11	**in streets of London, '63**
Sun.	12	Lord Rodney's Victory, 1782
Mon.	13	"Coomassie," 1868
Tue.	14	**Tiger and Pearl Matches**
Wed.	15	**first exported, 1866**
Thu.	16	"Culloden," 1746
Fri.	17	**Amorphous Phosp. disc., '45**
Sat.	18	Aldershot Camp estd., 1854
Sun.	19	Lord Beaconsfield d., 1881
Mon.	20	**Match Tax proposed, 1871**
Tue.	21	**"Promethean" Match, '30**
Wed.	22	**Gt. sensation in Country '71**
Thu.	23	Shakespeare d., 1616
Fri.	24	**Matchmakers' march, 1871**
Sat.	25	**Match Tax withdrawn, '71**
Sun.	26	Fire at Whiteley's, 1884
Mon.	27	W. C. Macready d., 1873
Tue.	28	Mutiny of the Bounty, 1789
Wed.	29	T. A. Trollope b., 1810
Thu.	30	Sir John Lubbock b., 1834

2.11 Express Dairies gave away a pop-up model of an ideal kitchen where children and kittens were fattening up on milk

2.10 This Bryant and May Almanack uses quotes from Shakespeare in the punning idiom beloved of the Victorians

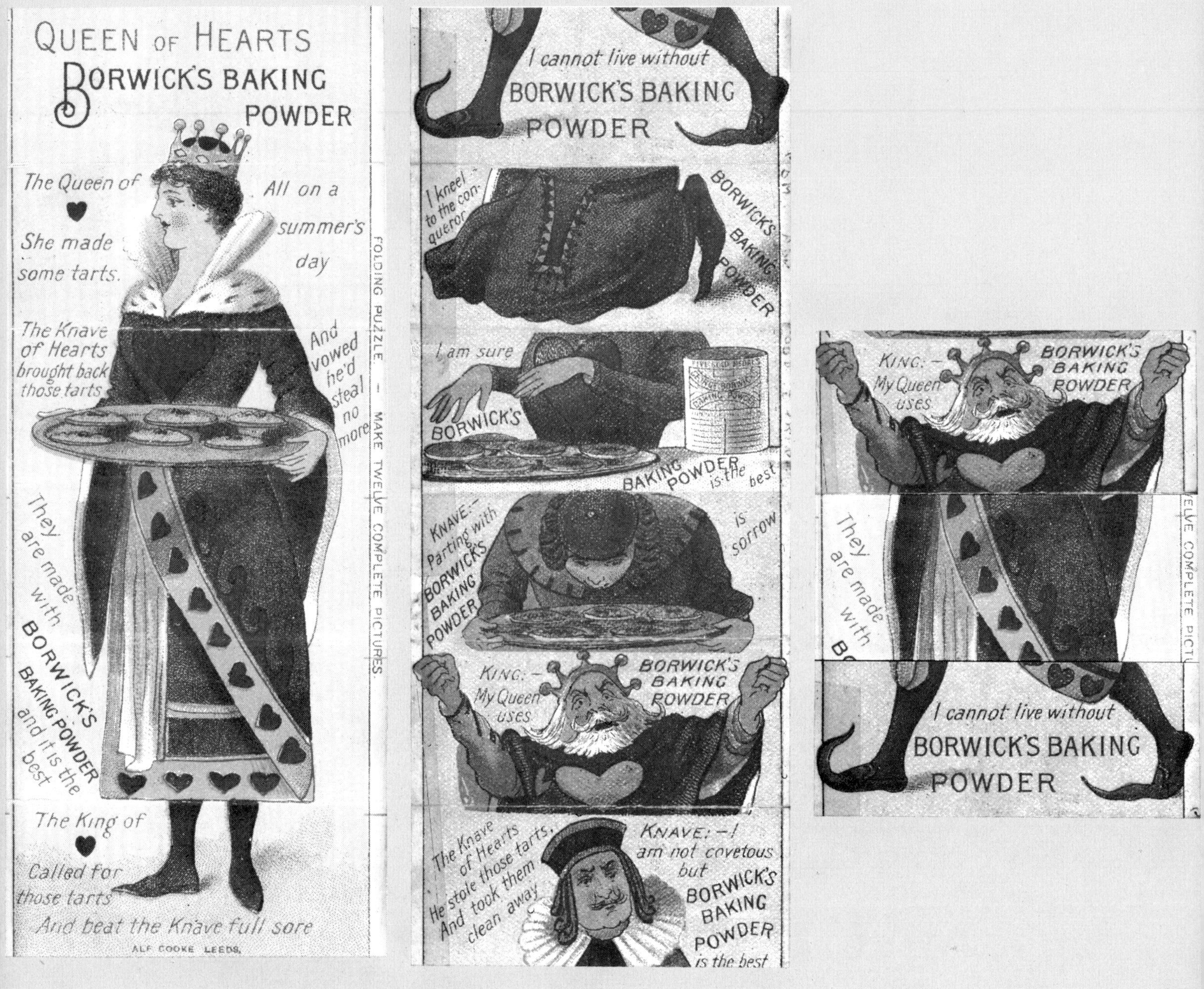

2.12 Puzzles delighted the Victorian consumer. This folding game from Borwicks made twelve pictures illustrating the nursery rhyme and plugging the manufacturer's name

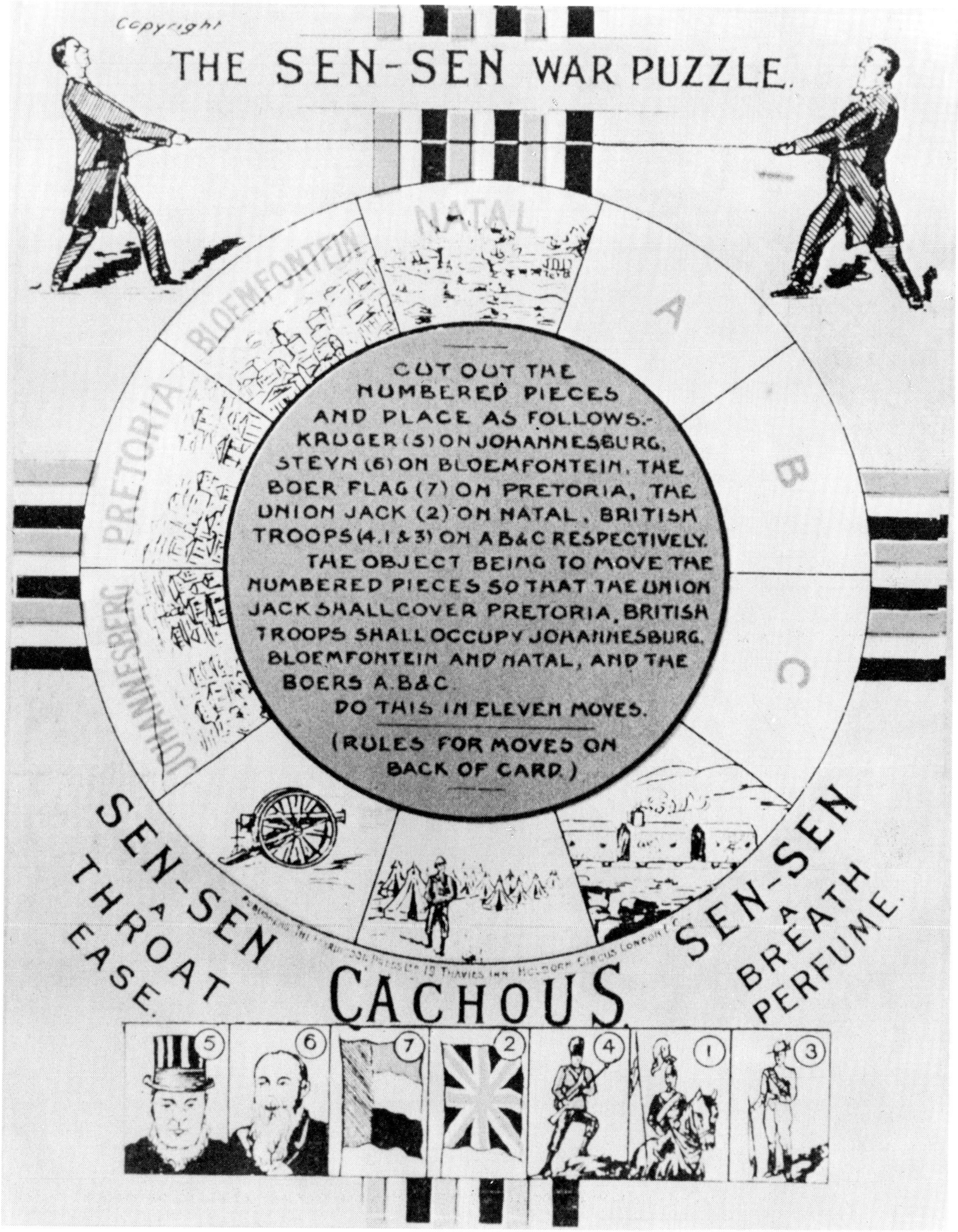

2.13 The aim of this puzzle was to move the counters so that the British forces occupied the strategic points and the Boer leaders landed up in a prison camp – a somewhat easier puzzle than the Boer War proved for the British Army

2.14 Producing copies of attractive posters for collectors was another way of promoting a product

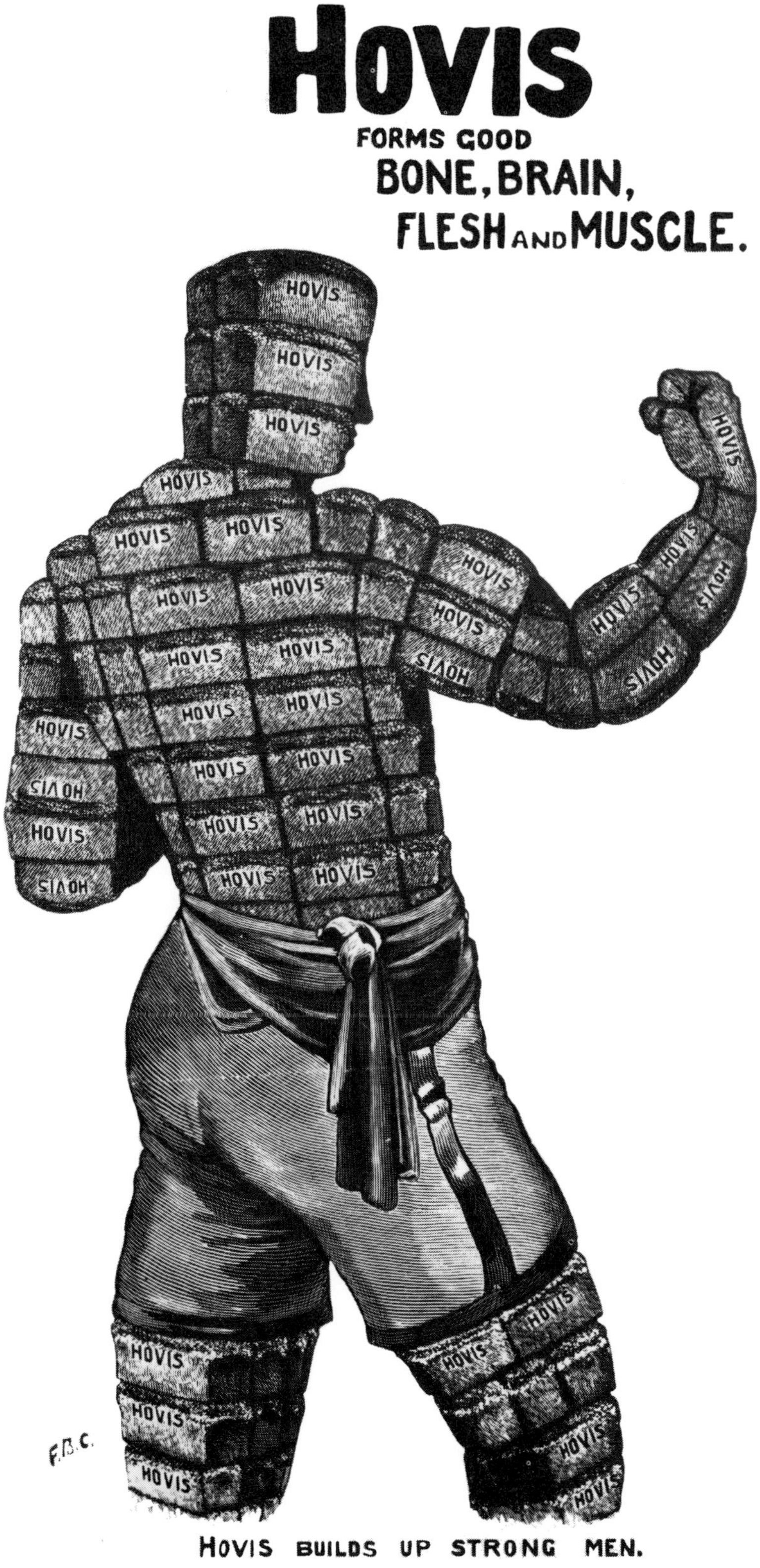

3.1 An early robot built with Hovis!

3.2 One of several attractive posters done for Colmans by John Hassall

3.3 Another poster by John Hassall, showing his strong graphic style

3.4 This magnificent poster by the "Beggarstaff Brothers" (artists James Pryde and William Nicholson) heralded a new spirit of simplicity and artistic quality in advertising

3.5 This fire engine was in the forefront of technological development in the 1890's. Cadbury's, like many advertisers today, wanted to identify their product with modern images

3.6 The copy line of this advertisement stresses the drink's medicinal properties – always a strong selling line for cocoa in the 19th century

3.7 Dicken's novels, like many other 19th century works, came out in weekly parts which carried advertisements in special sections at the back like this

No. VI.—August, 1852.

BLEAK HOUSE ADVERTISER.

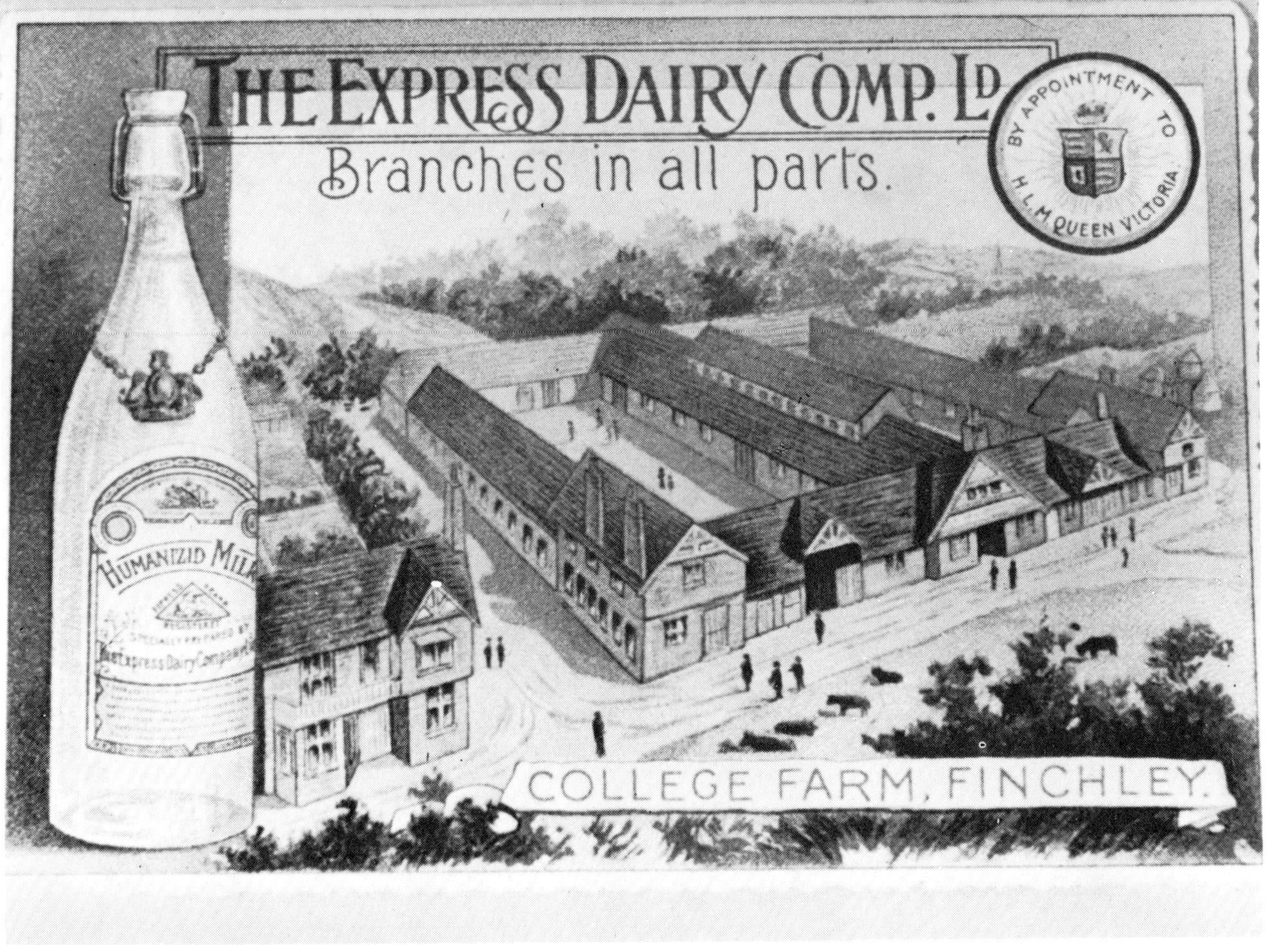
THE EXPRESS DAIRY COMP. Ld
Branches in all parts.
BY APPOINTMENT TO H.L.M. QUEEN VICTORIA
HUMANIZED MILK
COLLEGE FARM, FINCHLEY.

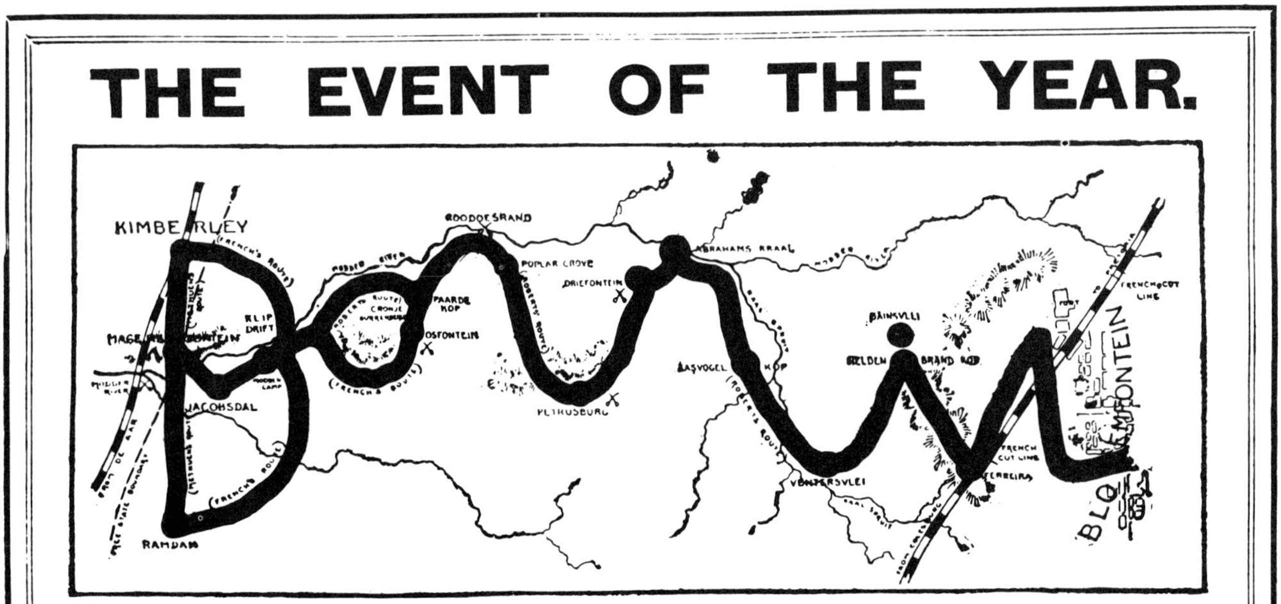
THE EVENT OF THE YEAR.
How Lord Roberts wrote BOVRIL.
Careful examination of this Map will show that the route followed by Lord Roberts in his historical march to Kimberley and Bloemfontein has made an indelible imprint of the word Bovril on the face of the Orange Free State.
This extraordinary coincidence is one more proof of the universality of Bovril, which has already figured so conspicuously throughout the South African Campaign.
Whether for the Soldier on the Battlefield, the Patient in the Sick-room, the Cook in the Kitchen, or for those as yet in full health and strength at home, Bovril is Liquid Life.

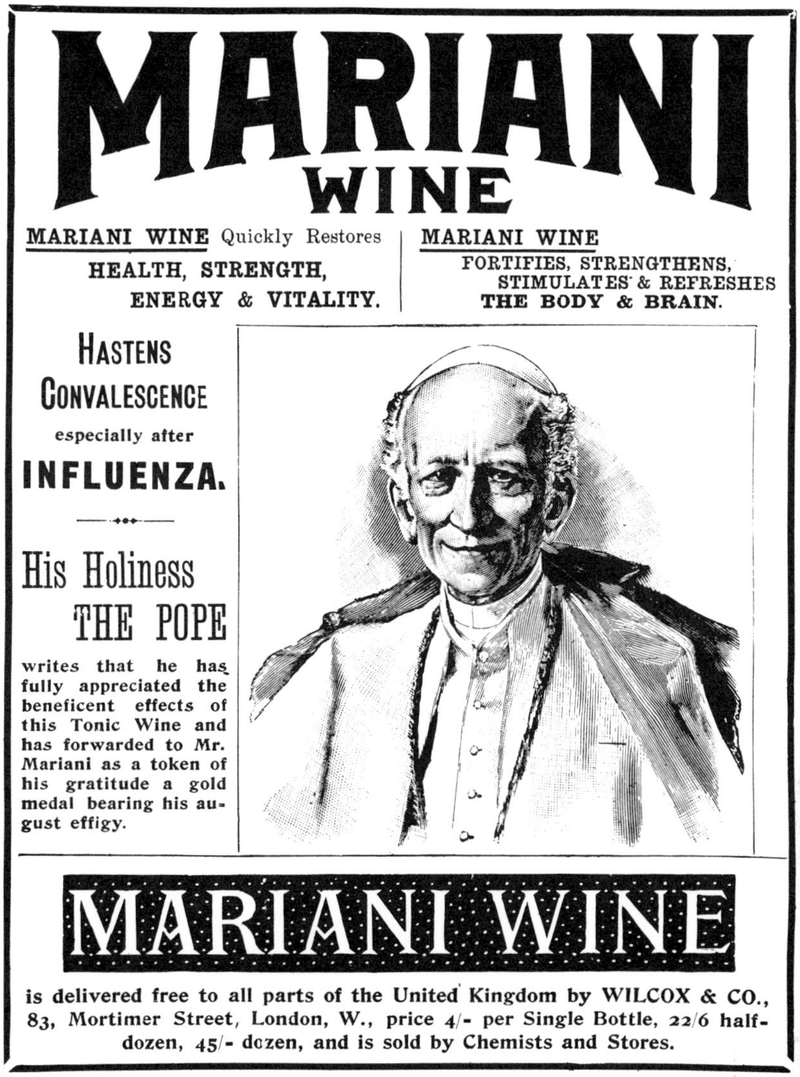

3.10 Even in Protestant England the papacy exercised a fascination. After the declaration of Papal Infallibility in 1870 the ad-men had another pun to play with

3.11 Pope Leo XII was one of the most forward looking popes of modern times. A fact no doubt fully confirmed for the makers of Mariani wines when he sent a gold medal to their founder as testimonial to the product

3.8 A much-favoured formula of advertisers was to depict the factory where a product was made; reasonably enough, a dairy saw a model farm as something to boast about

3.9 During the Boer War Bovril made great play with the fact that their product was standard issue for the troops. The alert ad-man who spotted the word 'Bovril' in Lord Robert's route must have earned himself promotion

3.12 This illustration by "Phiz" for Dickens immensely popular novel *Pickwick Papers* was, of course, a godsend for Guinness's copywriters

3.13 The fine monumental lettering of this Guinness advertisement shows that the company's outstanding advertising has a long tradition

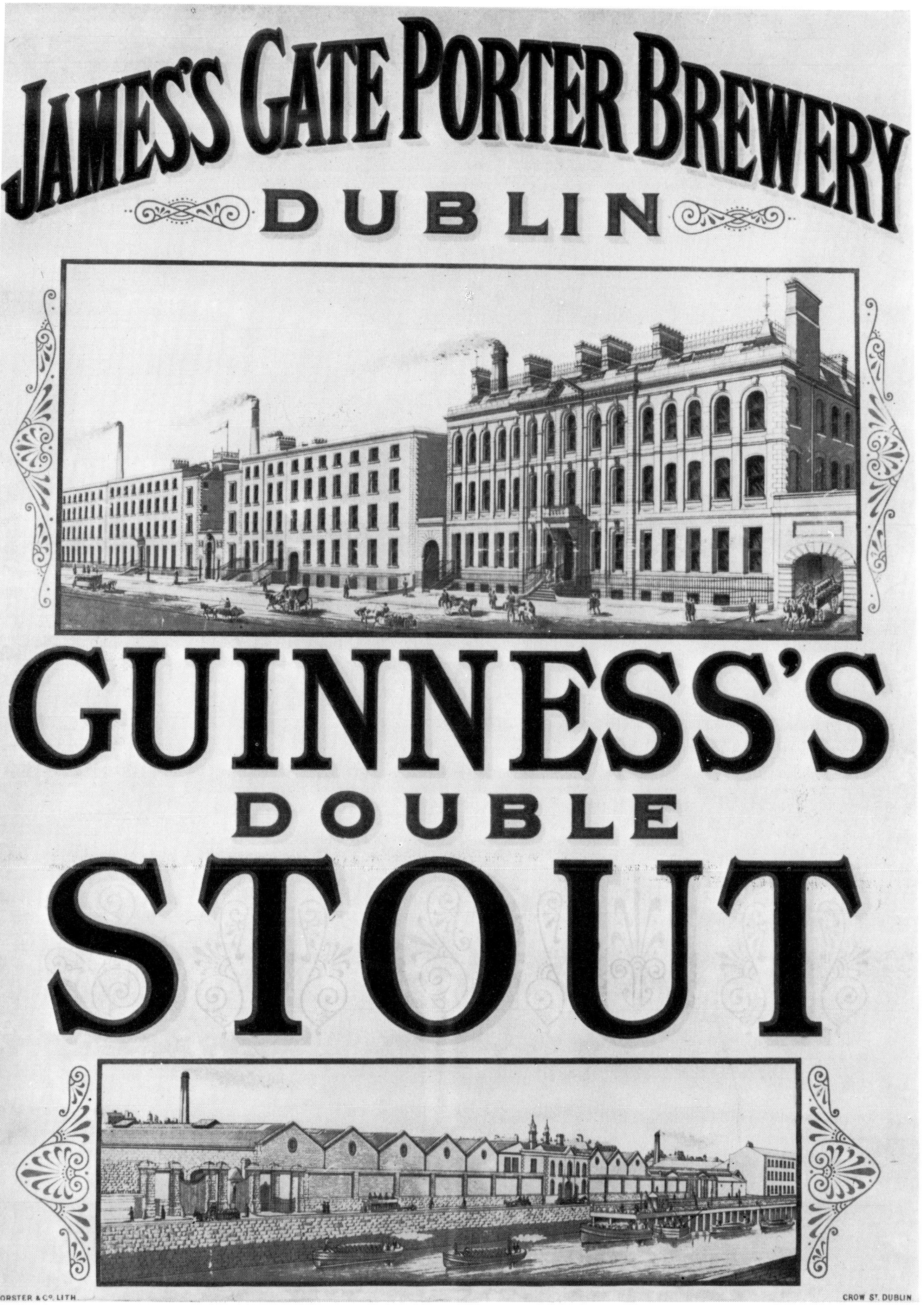
JAMES'S GATE PORTER BREWERY
DUBLIN
GUINNESS'S
DOUBLE
STOUT
FORSTER & Co. LITH.
CROW St. DUBLIN

Heartsease Cigarettes
W. D. & H. O. Wills.

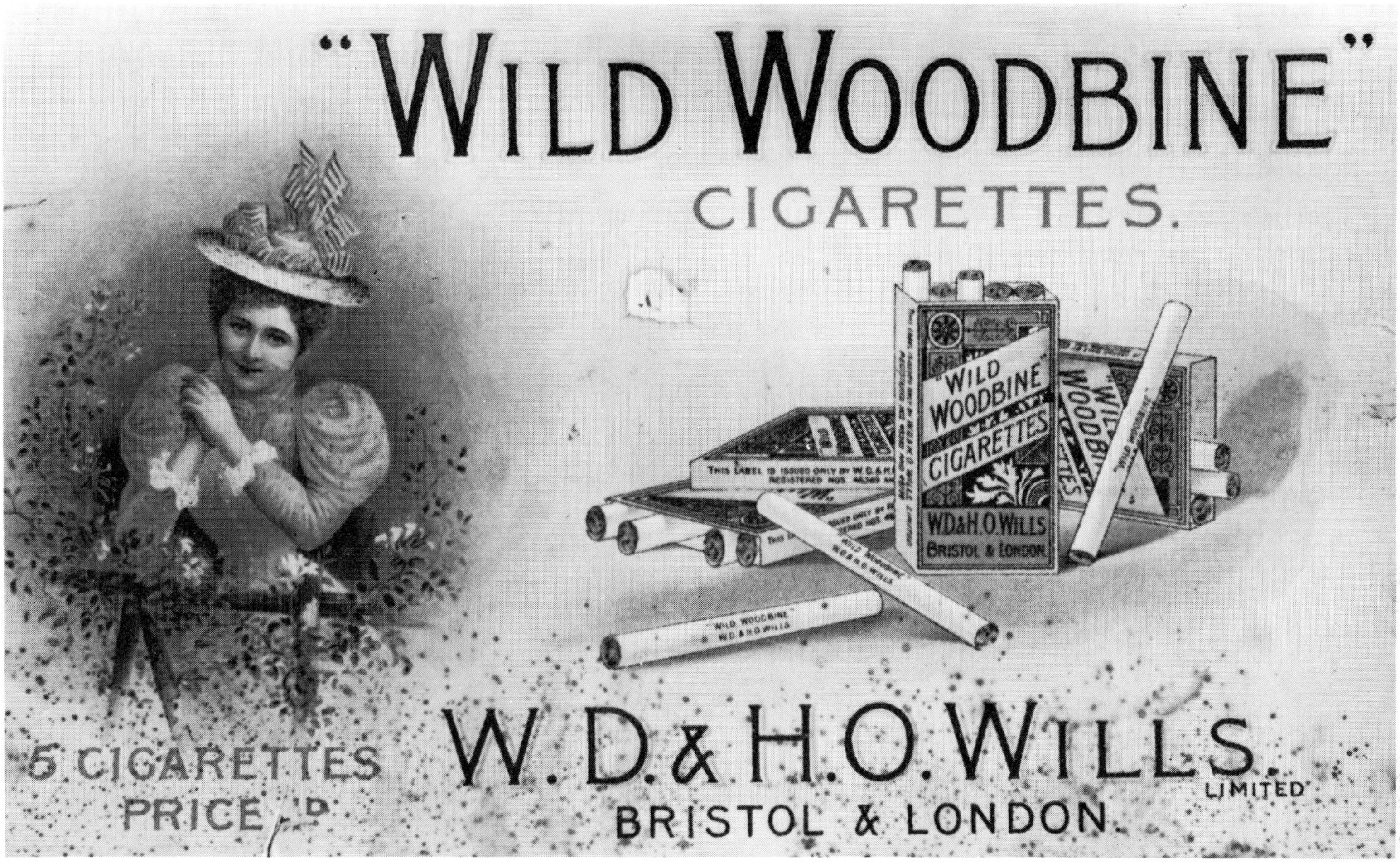

4.2 A "Wild Woodbine" could no doubt be a heartsease too

4.1 The merest hint of sex in this advertisement for Heartsease cigarettes was an omen of what the advertising business was going to do with that commodity in the coming century

THE ONLY COMFORT IN KLONDYKE
See these nuggets?
I'd give the lot for another tin of
WILLS'S "CAPSTAN"
WILLS'S "CAPSTAN"
(NAVY CUT)
W.D.& H.O. WILLS. L^TD
BRISTOL & LONDON
MEDIUM STRENGTH
CAPSTAN
Navy Cut
W.D.& H.O. WILLS.
Bristol & London.

4.3 The Klondyke Gold Rush, not surprisingly, fascinated advertisers. This window showcard for Wills' tobacco exploited it neatly

4.4 An old story, but a modern copywriter would have made more of the fact that the company had taken the name of Sir Walter Raleigh's country home

4.5 Dudley Hardy was one of the outstanding poster artists of the period. At the turn of the century the Phillips company was involved in a mammoth advertising war with Ogdens, each company taking as many as four pages in the London evening press at a time

5 ADVERTISEMENTS FOR PILLS AND POTIONS

CONTEMPLATION IS THE ONLY LASTING PLEASURE.

THE DAWN OF ANOTHER DAY.

"Out of eternity this new day is born;
Into eternity at night doth return;
Behold it aforetime, no eyes ever did,
So soon it for ever from all eyes is hid.
Here hath been dawning another blue day.
Think, wilt thou let it slip useless away?"

TO THE WISE.
Nor love thy life, nor hate;
But what thou livest live well."—Milton.

TO THE FOOLISH.
A man without wisdom lives in a fool's paradise.

ADVICE TO WOULD-BE SUICIDES.—POLITICS, &c.—Many hold their lives so cheap as to commit the terrible crime of suicide. Instead, however, of recklessly attaining that end by poison, the rope, pistol, or knife, &c., we recommend the following modes—as being more natural, and quite as effectual:—Wear thin shoes on damp nights, and keep every apartment air-tight. Keep the mind in a round of unnatural excitement, by politics (to enable you to produce election fever), trashy novels, and gambling speculations, either on cards, races, or stock. Go to operas, minstrel concerts, theatres in all sorts of weather, and, when steaming hot with perspiration, rush into the cold air with your coat or shawl hanging over your arm. In balls, dance till exhausted, and then go home in your pumps through the damp streets and air. Sleep on feather beds in the smallest and closest room in the house. Eat immoderately of hot and stimulating diet. Never drink anything weaker than strong tea, nor anything stronger than neat whiskey or brandy. Teach your children early to drink strong coffee, chew or smoke tobacco. Marry in a hurry, and growl and repent for the rest of your life. Never masticate food, but bolt it like a serpent. Follow any exciting or unhealthy business, if money can be made at it, so that your friends may console themselves for your early death. Never go to bed before midnight, and then with a full stomach. Eat little niceties, such as pastries, unripe fruit, lunch, wine, &c., between meals. Be always in a passion, either of anger or love.

When ailing, pay no attention to the regulation of your diet, exercise, or occupation. Always avoid ENO'S FRUIT SALT. Attempt no conformity to the laws of life, but gormandise to your uttermost bent, and you will be surprised to learn of the body what—

A frail and fickle tenement it is,
Which, like the brittle glass that measures time,
Is often broke ere half its sands are run.

ENO'S FRUIT SALT versus BRANDY.—"There were a few attacks of mild dysentery, brought mainly on by ill-considered devotion to brandy, or biliousness produced by the same cause. For the latter we used to swear by ENO'S FRUIT SALT, which is simply invaluable."—See "Coral Lands," Vol. I.

WHAT HIGHER AIM CAN MAN ATTAIN THAN CONQUEST OVER HUMAN PAIN?

Don't be without a Bottle of

ENO'S FRUIT SALT.

BILE-LADEN BLOOD.—Healthy Bile.—When the liver is not making healthy bile, or insufficient quantity, the blood becomes impure—the groundwork of disease—and produces constipation, dyspepsia, biliousness, headaches, &c. ENO'S FRUIT SALT is the best remedy.

BUSINESS AND PLEASURE.—"Having come out here on business and pleasure several days ago, and having had a very severe and protracted passage from England, whereby the whole of us were prostrated by sea-sickness in its most severe form, and after being here a few days, we set out to visit the Hot Springs, and on our return hence the reaction of the sea-sickness, combined with the change of living, began to tell upon us. We were troubled with flatulency, biliousness, nausea, and giddiness, which rendered us rather miserable, and one of our party being provided with pills, we took several, but without any result. Strolling through the small town, one of us happened, accidentally, to see a bottle of ENO'S FRUIT SALT in the window of a store, and we immediately went and purchased it. We can assure you that this seemed an unexpected blessing, for we knew its good qualities well enough to know that we had a medicine which at least we could rely upon for setting us up again. We have had two doses before breakfast yesterday and to-day, and the effect is really wonderful. All traces of headache, biliousness, &c., have passed away, and we are in first-class spirits, and able to appreciate and see with pleasure the wonderful vagaries of nature in this district. We can unhesitatingly recommend your preparation to all who may be similarly afflicted, and trust that it may meet with a still wider sale, as its good and excellent qualities fully entitle it.

"Mr. ENO, London. "TRUTH, Reykjavik, Iceland, Oct. 9."

STIMULANTS and insufficient amount of exercise frequently derange the liver. ENO'S FRUIT SALT is peculiarly adapted for any constitutional weakness of the liver. A world of woes is avoided by those who keep and use ENO'S FRUIT SALT. "All our Customers for ENO'S FRUIT SALT would not be without it upon any consideration, they having received so much benefit from it.—WOOD BROS, Chemists, Jersey, 1878."

CAUTION.—Legal rights are protected in every civilised country. Read the following:—"In the Supreme Court of Sydney (N.S.W.) an appeal from a decree of Sir W. Manning perpetually restraining the Defendant (Hogg) from selling a fraudulent imitation of ENO'S FRUIT SALT, and giving heavy damages to the Plaintiff, has, after a most exhaustive trial of two days' duration, been unanimously dismissed with costs."—Sydney Morning Herald, Nov. 28.

Examine each Bottle, and see that the capsule is marked ENO'S FRUIT SALT. Without it you have been imposed on by a worthless imitation. Sold by all Chemists.

PREPARED ONLY AT ENO'S FRUIT SALT WORKS, HATCHAM, LONDON, S.E., BY J. C. ENO'S PATENT.

5.1, 5.2 Two typical Eno advertisements

THE GRAND OLD MAGICIAN'S IRISH POLICY.

A WONDERFUL REMEDY No settlement of any question, great or small, can be equitable and permanent which is not approached by all concerned in a perfectly unprejudiced spirit; no person who is in any way affected in health can be for long in a truly unbiassed and judicial frame of mind; therefore—to secure a lasting and satisfactory settlement of the **GREAT IRISH PROBLEM** it is absolutely necessary that the whole English-speaking race should be able to bring the full powers of the mind to bear upon the subject, untrammelled by any disease or ill-humours of the body.

To gain this end there is no better means than **BEECHAM'S PILLS,** which are well known to carry off all the gross humours and impurities of the system, and thus, by sweeping and garnishing the temple of the soul, set the mind free to bring all its powers to bear on this, the most momentous question of modern times. Sold everywhere, in Boxes, 1s. 1½d. and 2s. 9d.

5.3 Topicality was highly rated and current affairs offered a natural field of operation for many advertisements. Whether or not the cartoon in this advertisement was intended as an attack on Gladstone's Irish policy, it certainly brought the name of Beechams before the public

5.4 Women's suffrage movements of the early 20th century were preceded by a wave of women's liberation in the 1880's and 1890's. The new woman paraded her emancipation in the face of shock and then derision from conservatives of both sexes. Beechams cashed in with the kind of joke that Victorians found highly entertaining

5.5 When the Prince of Wales' ship sailed into Bombay Harbour in 1891 Beechams exploited the occasion brilliantly

5.6 Another reminder that Beecham's were used throughout the empire

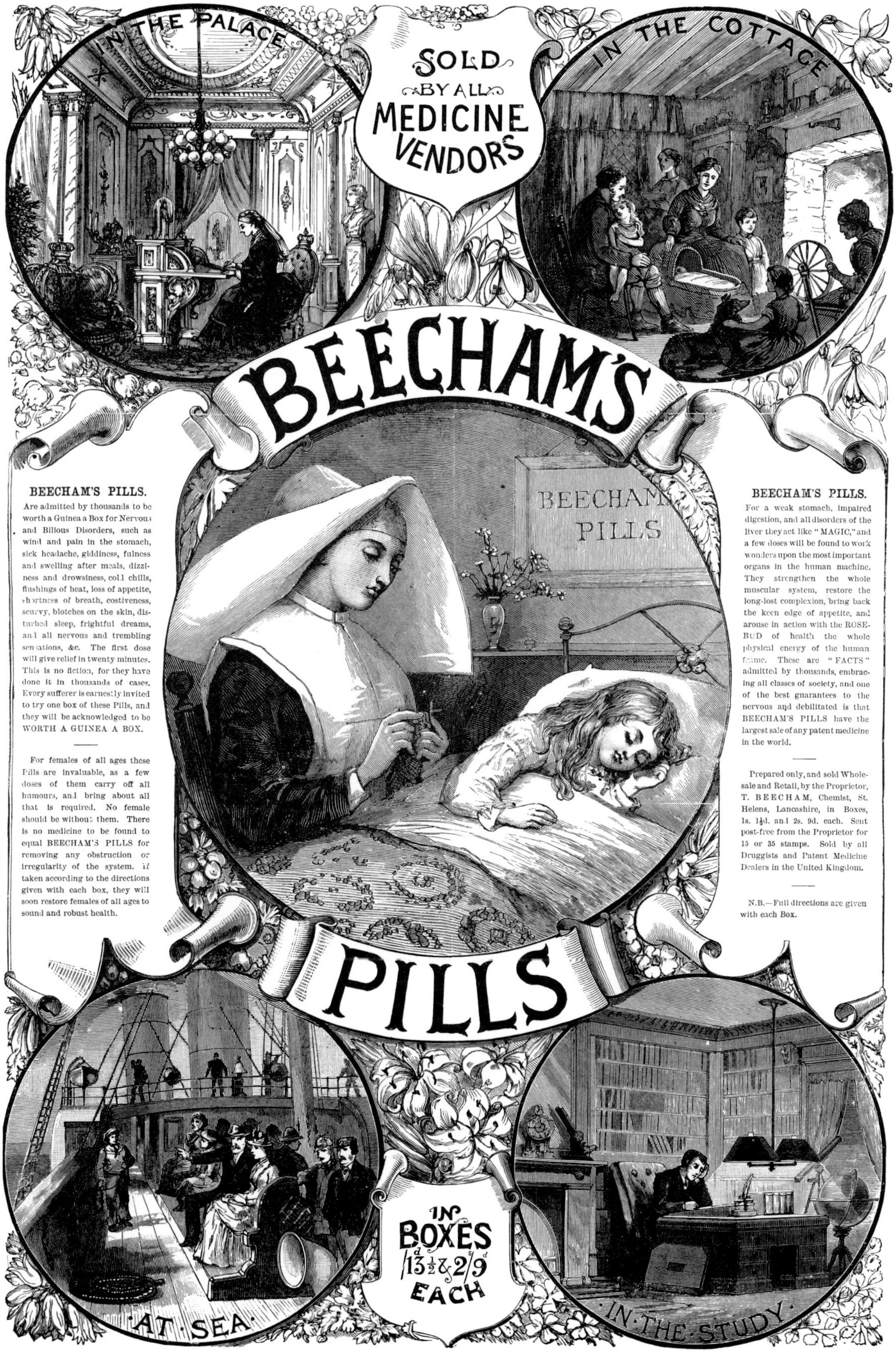

5·7 A full-page prestige advertisement for Beecham's – even Queen Victoria takes second place to the message that the pills are essential at the sick bed

ELLIMAN'S 1/1½
UNIVERSAL EMBROCATION
RHEUMATISM LUMBAGO SPRAINS
UNIVERSAL ELLIMAN'S EMBROCATION
BRUISES CHEST COLDS
STIFFNESS 1/1½
"IT I WILL HAVE OR I WILL HAVE NONE"
Prepared only by ELLIMAN Sons. & Co. Slough England.
FOR STIFFNESS. ACHES. SPRAINS. BRUISES.

5.8 Elliman's, like many other advertisers, eagerly caught on to the cycling craze at the end of the century

5.9 Like Enos and many others, Holloway occasionally sponsored prestige advertising for their pills; remarkably, however, the name of the product appears only on the back of decorative magazine inserts such as this one. But the message of Health and Purity is clear enough

6 SOAP AND COSMETICS ADVERTISEMENTS

6.1 Pears' Soap, one of the most famous names in the history of English advertising. The company made much of testimonials from the famous, Lillie Langtry the Prince of Wales's mistress and Adelina Patti the opera singer featuring their signatures and enthusiasm for the product year after year. The Harry Furniss cartoon in Punch became a nationwide joke and, following the principle that all publicity is good publicity, Pears themselves used it in advertising material

6.2 This Pears advertisement was the cause of another lampoon, this time a particularly vicious attack on Gladstone, showing him as the baby needing his bottom wiped

PEARS' SOAP
A SPECIALTY FOR INFANTS

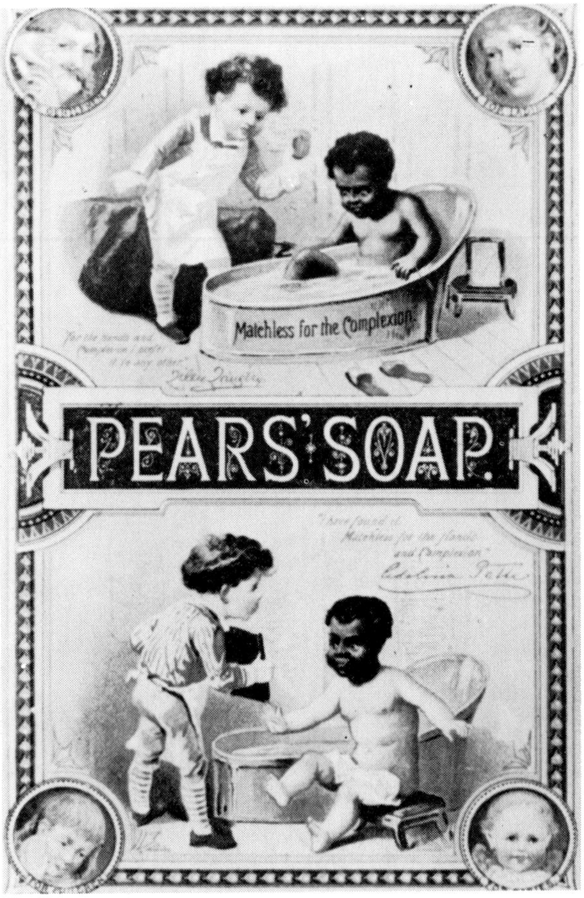

6.3 A telling advertisement no doubt in the days before Black was Beautiful

6.4 Another potent image from Pears advertising men. If the English obsession with cleanliness made them the laughing stock of Europe it was to them a proof of their superior civilization

6.5 Printing techniques were not advanced enough to allow colour in the average magazine and their bright colours therefore made these little inserts doubly popular. Other examples are reproduced in the colour section of this book

SWAN
WHITE FLOATING
SOAP
MANUFACTURED BY
LEVER BROTHERS LIMITED.
PORT SUNLIGHT, CHESHIRE.

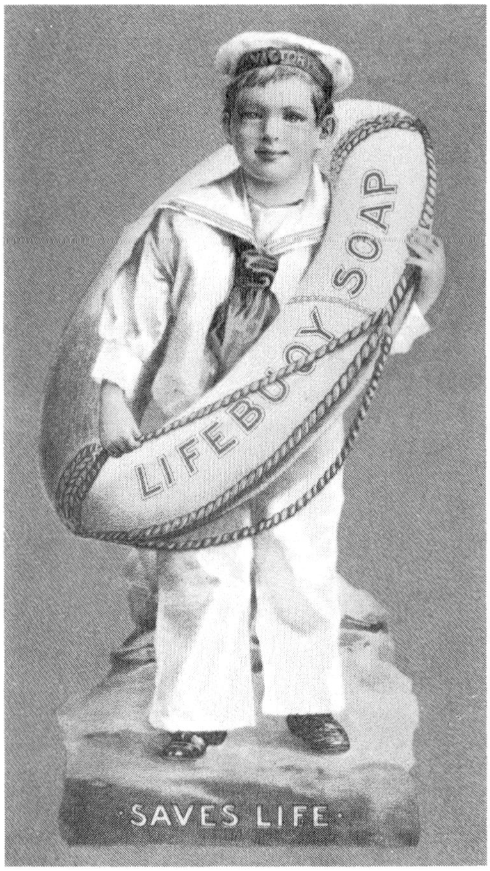

6.6 In an age less rich in picture material than ours, advertising cards like these, inserted in magazines, were often collected and even used as room decoration

6.7 The girly ad. was another type pioneered by the Victorians
6.8 This kind of elaborate engraving was costly to produce and, by the taste of the day, highly artistic; a good example of prestige advertising

6.9 The Victorians liked women to have long hair; Edward's Harlene had a ready sale

6.10 Whatever she may have suffered at the hands of the profligate Prince of Wales, her husband, Princess Alexandra could surely have been spared having herself publicly identified with a toothpaste

6.11 Rowlands, another cosmetic firm with roots in the 18th century, advertised consistently but usually discreetly. Beside Kalydor for the complexion, their range included Odonto for the teeth and the notorious Macassar oil for the hair. To combat its ravages on their furniture Victorian ladies spent hours working antimacassars to drape over the backs of chairs and sofas

7.1 Part of a series on sports by Freeman, Hardy and Willis. Underarm bowling had been standard until the 1820's, but 50 years later, the time of this advertisement, it was already contemptuously known as "lobbing"

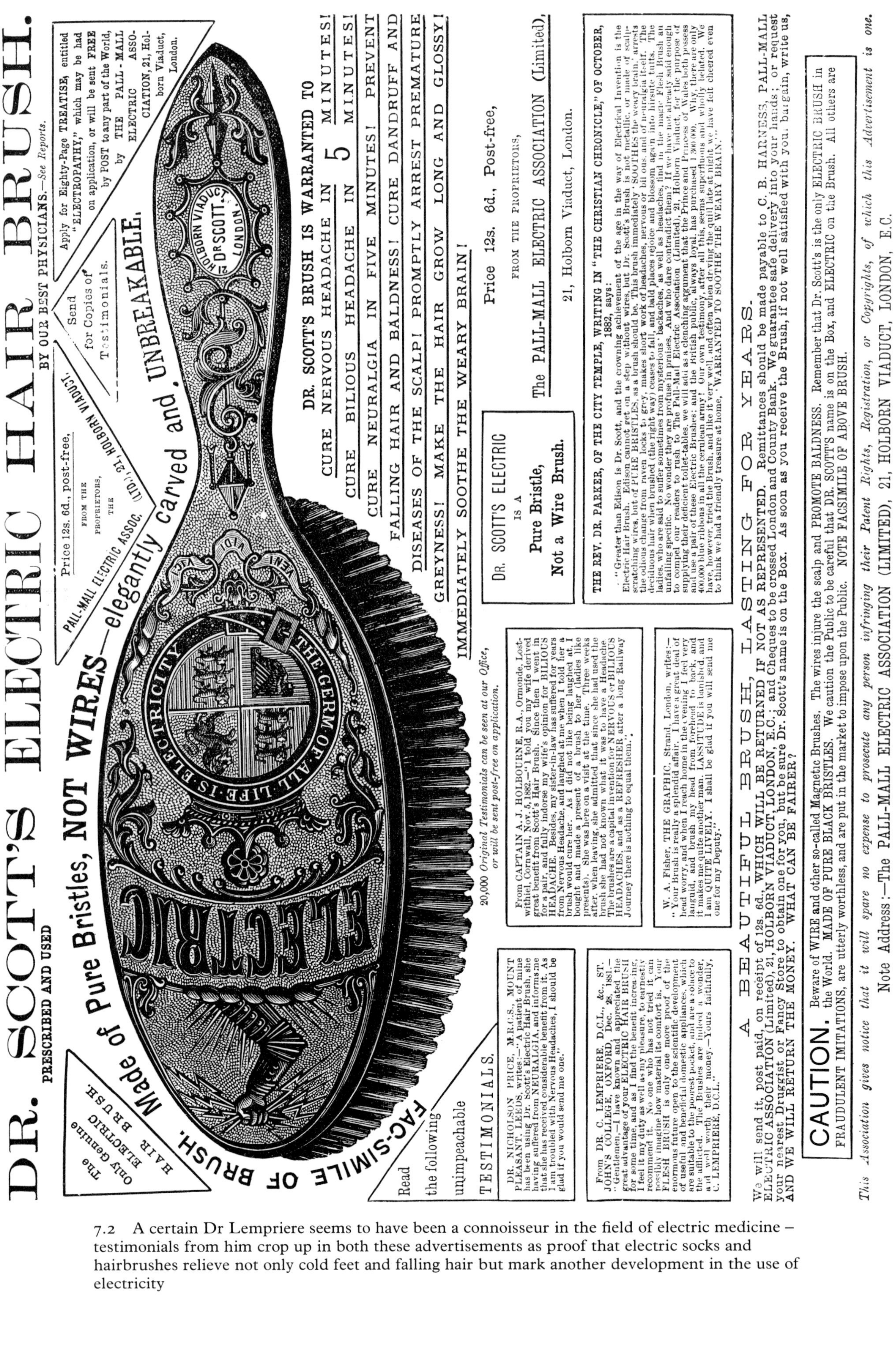

7.2 A certain Dr Lempriere seems to have been a connoisseur in the field of electric medicine – testimonials from him crop up in both these advertisements as proof that electric socks and hairbrushes relieve not only cold feet and falling hair but mark another development in the use of electricity

"THE ELECTRICPATENT SOCKS."

For creating a constant Electric Current and producing a high degree of warmth.

AN ABSOLUTE AND POSITIVE REMEDY

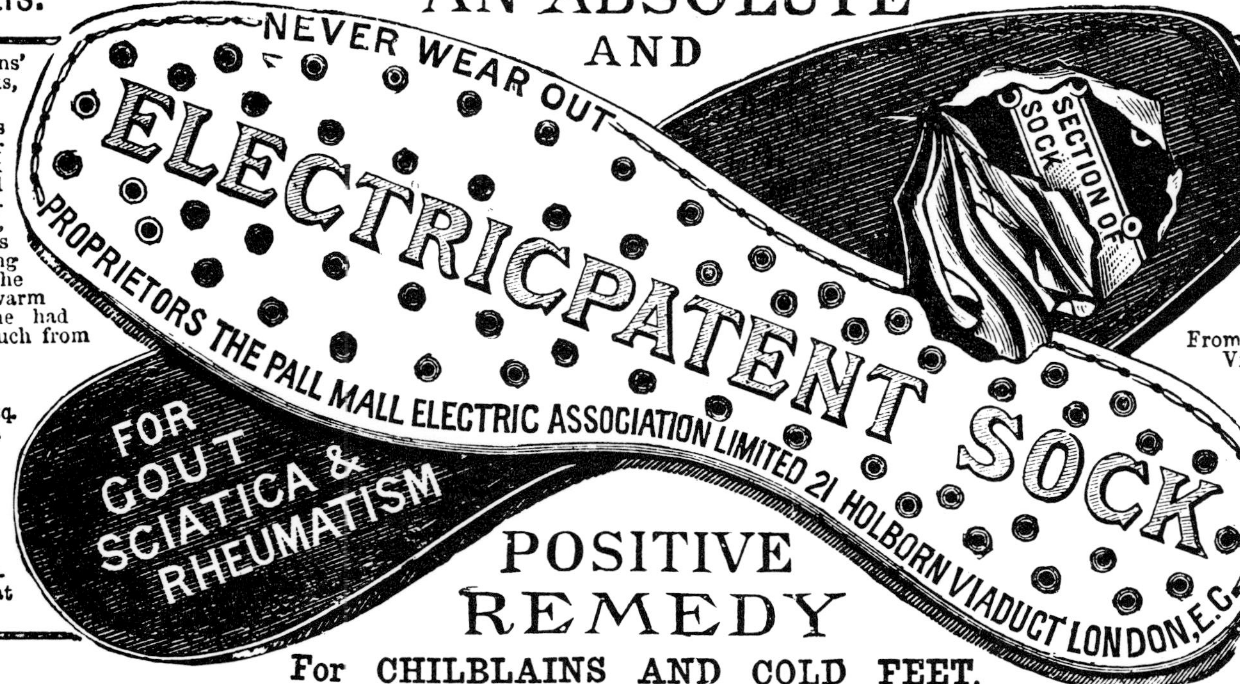

Testimonials.

From Miss Elam, Thorns' Hall, Sedbergh, Yorks, October 13th, 1882.

"Miss Elam encloses a Post Office Order for 12s 6d, and will thank Mr. Harness to send her a pair of the Electric Socks for a friend, size No. 2. Since Miss Elam has been wearing those sent, she finds he feet are wonderfully warm and comfortable. She had previously suffered much from cold feet."

From T. L. Selling, Esq. Royal Hotel, Ross, Herefordshire, Sept. 11th, 1882.

"I have had one of your Galvanic Generators, and a pair of your Electric Socks, from which I have experienced very great relief."

Testimonials.

From Dr. C. Lempriere, D.C.L., &c., January 20th, 1882.

"Your Electropathic Socks are indeed a wonder and a solace to those suffering from Gout, and another proof of the great future which is open to the scientific development of Electricity."

From Rev. R. Taylor, Twyford Vicarage, Melton Mowbray.

"Gentlemen,—Please send me circular of Dr. Scott's Electric Flesh Brush and appliances for the arms when affected with shaking or tremulousness. I recommended your Socks to a lady, who has found great benefit in them.

Yours truly.

R. Taylor."

For CHILBLAINS AND COLD FEET.

The SOCKS are simply put inside the shoes or boots, and after wearing them a short time a continued and most beneficial warmth penetrates the body.

These ELECTRIC SOCKS prove the best means for keeping the feet warm, for creating bodily comfort, and preventing illness; they are preventives against Rheumatism, Sciatica, and Gout. Chilblains, &c., and also are very beneficial in the first stages of spinal affections, &c. Although the Medical Faculty may disagree upon the true nature of Rheumatic Gout it is beyond doubt that in most cases the most effective remedy is electricity, which can best be conveyed into the system by the use of these Socks worn in boots.

The ELECTRIC SOCKS produce a current acting congenially on the body, and is far superior to the prickling and disagreeable influence of an induction coil. Against spinal complaints, the first symptoms of which are numbness of the feet and pricking sensation (so-called "Pins and Needles"), they act very effectively, the electric current influencing the spine through the peripheric ends of the nerves.

ELECTRIC SOCKS should be worn by those who have Rheumatic or Gouty Affections in the Feet, or are liable to coldness or chilblains in those parts. The circulation is at once stimulated, and an agreeable warmth diffused. The heat of the body causes Thermo-Electricity, the perspiration of the body evolves a galvanic current, and the Electric power is always in force.

IMPORTANCE OF WEARING ELECTRIC SOCKS.—Few are conscious of the very great advantage of wearing under the feet a medium that will not only prevent the abstraction of electricity by cold earth, but will at the same time generate in the feet those electric currents on which warmth depends.

Please forward Exact Size of Feet when ordering these Socks. All Chemists keep the Electricpatent Socks.

CAUTION.—**Beware of the rubbishy, so called magnetic socks that are sometimes stocked by Chemists on account of their low price—they cannot generate Electricity and are dear at any price. The Electricpatent Socks are only sold IN BOXES.**

Pair of Socks forwarded, post free, on receipt of Post Office Order or Cheque for **12s. 6d.**, to be made payable to **C. B. HARNESS**, Managing Director, **PALL MALL ELECTRIC ASSOCIATION, LTD, 21, HOLBORN VIADUCT, LONDON, E.C.**

7.3 Lillie Langtry, the actress, lent her name to advertise this cumbersome item of the Victorian lady's wardrobe

7.4 Two inventive aids for the Victorian male

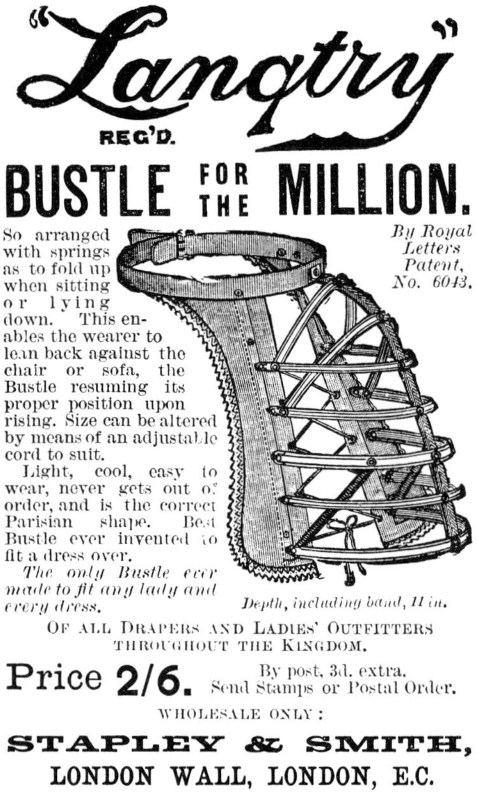

7.5 Then as now the market for domestic goods was one of the largest. The advantages of pure water were obvious enough at a time when it was still something of a luxury. The dangers of incrustations by hard water may not have been so apparent but they were evidently considerable

MAIGNEN'S BENEFICIAL INVENTIONS!

Loaded with HONOURS!

PURE WATER

Look to the Water you Drink, and be Wary of Imperfect and Unsafe Filters.

MAIGNEN'S

PATENT

"Filtre-Rapide"

Is a certain protection against the insidious horrors that lurk in the domestic water supply. It is guaranteed to remove all germs of Cholera, Typhoid, Diphtheria, and all causes of Blood Poisoning, such as dissolved Sewage, Lead, Zinc, Copper, or other noxious Metals.

The LANCET says,—"A better Filter could not be desired."

Differing in its construction and arrangements from all other Filters, the "Filtre-Rapide" is simplicity itself, easy to manage, and under perfect control, while its deodorising and purifying powers are in excess of any others. It can be taken to pieces, cleansed, and re-charged in a few minutes by the users. The Filters are made in various sizes and kinds to suit all requirements, but the principle is the same throughout, viz:—A large filtering surface, not liable to decay or disintegration,—pure Asbestos Cloth, specially woven from picked fibre, coated with Maignen's Patent Carbo-Calcis.

VISCOUNT WOLSELEY writes:

"*I have much pleasure in stating that* MAIGNEN'S *Patent* 'FILTRE-RAPIDE' *which was used by our Troops in the Expedition up the Nile, gave very satisfactory results indeed. It filtered the water both quickly and well, and was much valued by our Soldiers.*

Wolseley

To be Filled by Hand. *For attaching to the Service Pipes.*

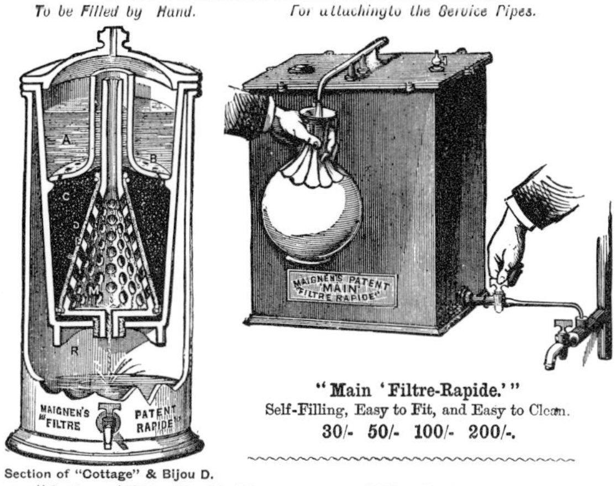

"Main 'Filtre-Rapide.'"
Self-Filling, Easy to Fit, and Easy to Clean.
30/- 50/- 100/- 200/-.

Section of "Cottage" & Bijou D.

"Cottage 'Filtre-Rapide.'" (Brown Stoneware.)
15/- 25/- 35/- 55/- 70/- 105/-

"Bijou D 'Filtre-Rapide.'" (Decorated White Stoneware.)
25/- 40/- 60/- 105/-

See Pamphlet for description of other classes of "FILTRES-RAPIDES—"TABLE" (Glass), from 3/6—"EXPORT" (Enamelled Iron), from 12/6.—"TAP" (Rustless Metal), from 12/6,—"TOURIST" (White Metal) from 18s.,—"WATCH" (Pocket Filter) from 10/6.

Large Supply for Village and Town Water-Works. Eight different Classes approved by the Government for the Army, &c., &c.

SOFT WATER

IN EVERY HOME.

MAIGNEN'S

PATENT

"Anti-Calcaire"

Renders the Hardest Spring or Town Water like the Softest Rain Water.

Everybody will welcome "ANTI-CALCAIRE" so manifold are the uses, blessings, comforts, luxuries, needs, and applications of a real WATER-SOFTENER. It is a perfectly harmless powder which attacks, decomposes, and precipitates all the Carbonates of Lime and Magnesia, and the Sulphate of Lime, leaving nothing injurious in the water.

HARD WATER is cruelly hurtful, wasteful, and destructive. It ruins the complexion, makes the hair harsh and brittle, causes roughness and irritability of the skin, is a nuisance and an injury all round, and should be avoided in all toilet, bath, nursery, domestic, cooking, cleansing, gardening, medicinal, and mechanical uses.

"To soften Hard Water," says THE QUEEN, "use MAIGNEN'S Patent 'ANTI-CALCAIRE' Powder—quite harmless and inexpensive."

Explosion due to Incrustations, caused by Hard Water, preventable by "Anti-Calcaire." For Testimonials see Pamphlet.

"ANTI-CALCAIRE" is sold by Chemists, Ironmongers, Grocers, and Oilmen, in Tins, with printed directions for the Toilet and other domestic uses, at 2d., 6d., 1s., 2s., 3s. 6d., & 7s. each; also in Casks by the Cwt. or Ton, for Laundries, Steam Boilers, and Water-Works, by the Inventor. A Sample Tin and Pamphlet sent for 5 stamps.

Read Pamphlet, Post-free, "Water, Preventable Disease and Filtration."

P. A. MAIGNEN, CONTRACTOR TO H.M. GOVERNMENT, 32, ST. MARY-AT-HILL, EASTCHEAP, E.C.; 15, PALL-MALL, S.W., LONDON.

Paris.—La Compagnie Générale de Filtrage des Eaux de la Ville de Paris, 83, Rue du Bac. | Brussels.—A. De Keyser, 75, Rue du Canal. Amsterdam.—J. C. Wolterbeek, 73, Reguliersdwarsstraat. | Copenhagen.—Hornum & Co., 13, St. Amiac Plades. St. Petersburg.—Gen. Lavroff and Prince Hynglatt-Gatschino.

7.6 Early hatching equipment

7.7 Another fine piece of design for Colmans

7.8 The monkey of the Monkey Brand soap was to be seen everywhere, on hoardings and in magazines. The idea of exploiting a negative quality as an advantage lay behind the slogan "Won't wash clothes"; the implication being, of course, that it would wash every other household object

7.9 Monkey Brand press advertisements detailing the benefits to be expected from using the soap

BROOKE'S SOAP MONKEY BRAND

Cleans Metals, Marble, Painted Surfaces, Windows, &c.

4D. A LARGE BAR.

SPOTLESS EARTHENWARE

SMILING HOUSEWIVES.

CLEAN BATHS

HAPPY HUSBANDS.

WHITE MARBLE

CONTENTED SERVANTS.

SHINING POTS & PANS

IN THE PARLOUR.

POLISHED STAIR-RODS

IN THE KITCHEN.

BRIGHT FIRE-IRONS

IN THE FACTORY.

SPARKLING GLASS-WARE

WON'T WASH CLOTHES!

CLEANS, SCOURS, SCRUBS, POLISHES, BRIGHTENS EVERYTHING.

For Oil-Cloths, Bicycles, Guns, Swords, Helmets, &c. For Soiled Hands.

NO DIRT. NO DUST. NO WASTE. NO LABOUR.

SIMPLE!! RAPID!! CLEAN!! CHEAP!!

Approved by **100** Leading Newspapers.

Sold by Grocers, Ironmongers, and Chemists. If not obtainable near you, send 7d. in stamps for full-sized Bar, free by post (1s. for two Bars, free by post), or 1d. stamp for Small Sample, free by post, mentioning this Paper, to

B. BROOKE & CO., 36 to 40, York-road, King's-cross, London, N.

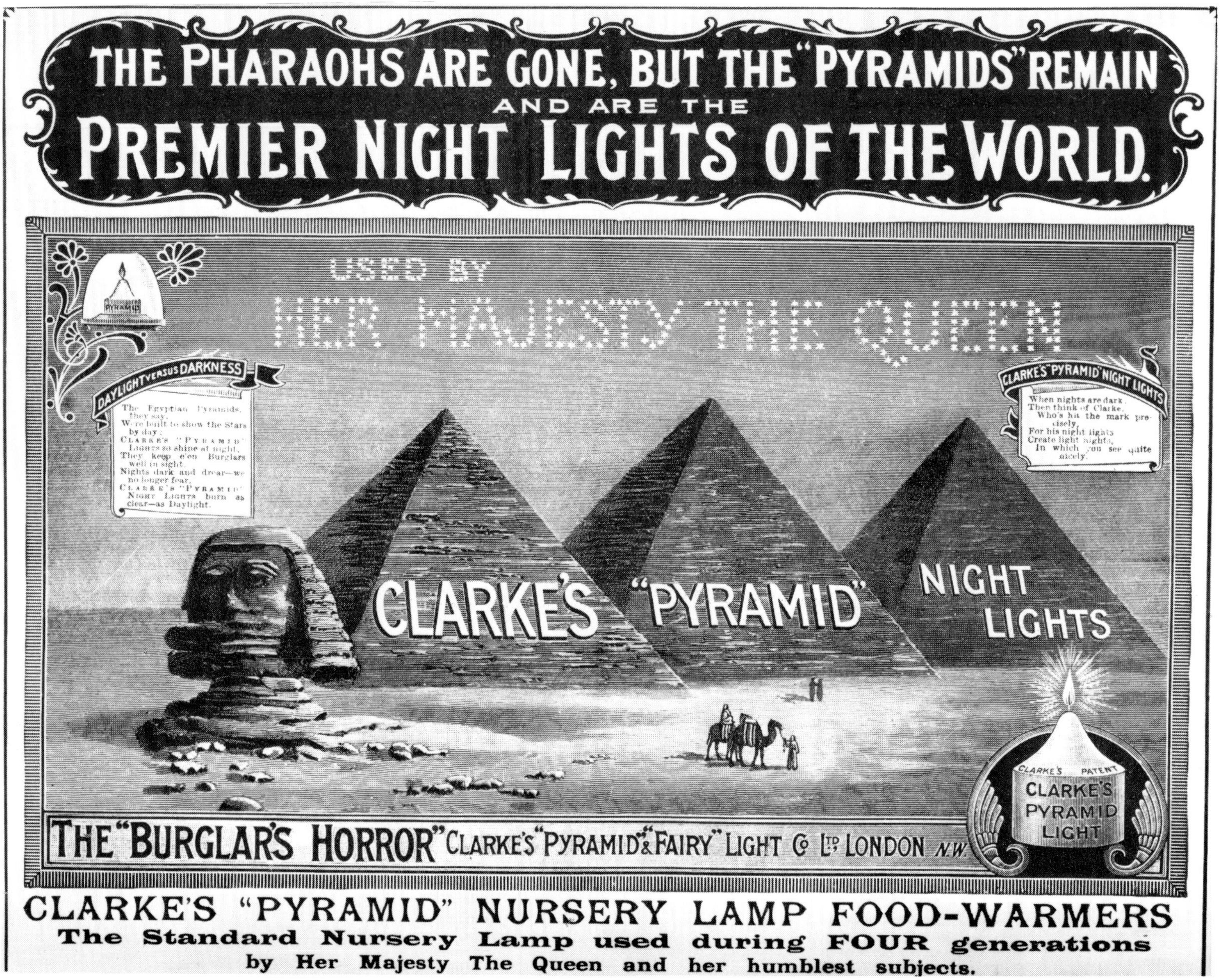

7.10 A dream to fire the imagination of any advertiser
7.11 Here the flame of patriotism burns bright!

UNITED AT LAST!

G.O.M.—"This Strop is simply grand."
Lord R. C.—"Yes; there is no opposition to that."

DO YOU SHAVE YOURSELF?
DOES YOUR RAZOR CUT?

The latter of these two questions will be easy to solve by stropping your Razor on

ESCOTT'S
PATENT
"ECLIPSE" SPRING DRAW-OUT
RAZOR STROP.

7.12 The Liberal Gladstone and the Tory Lord Randolph Churchill – political rivals but united in their agreement on the virtues of Escott's patent Eclipse razor strops
7.13 Another valuable invention for the domestic scene
7.14 "The course of a true love letter runs smoothest when written with one of C. Brandauer & Co's Circular Pointed Pens", runs the copy for this intriguing advertisement

THE PATENT SAFETY COT.

DEBENHAM and FREEBODY having purchased the exclusive right in the Patent Safety Folding and Elongating Cots, and made extensive arrangements for their manufacture, beg to introduce them to public notice. The Folding and Rocking Cot, illustrated, is made in tubular iron or brass, and combines STRENGTH and DURABILITY with LIGHTNESS and ELEGANCE, and is PERFECTLY SAFE. It can be used as a ROCKING COT, or by a simple adjustment can be rendered IMMOVABLE, and it will FOLD INTO A SMALL COMPASS for travelling or exportation. The Trimmed Cot forms a pretty article of furniture, and the entire construction renders it most conducive to the HEALTH, COMFORT, AND SAFETY OF CHILDREN.

Patent Folding and Rocking Iron Cots	..	..	No. 1	..	21s. 0d.
" " " "	(Tubular), recommended	"	2	..	25s. 0d.
" " " "	. "	"	3	..	57s. 6d.

TRIMMED COTS AT ESTIMATED PRICES.

SOLD·HERE
WALTER·CRANE'S
FLORAL·&·FANCIFUL
BOOKS·IN·COLOUR
VIZ:
FLORA'S FEAST
QUEEN SUMMER
A MASQUE OF DAYS
A FLOWER WEDDING
FLOWERS FROM SHAKESPEARE'S GARDEN
PRICE
FIVE·SHILLINGS
EACH
VOLUME
PUBLISHED·BY· CASSELL·&·CO:LIMD.

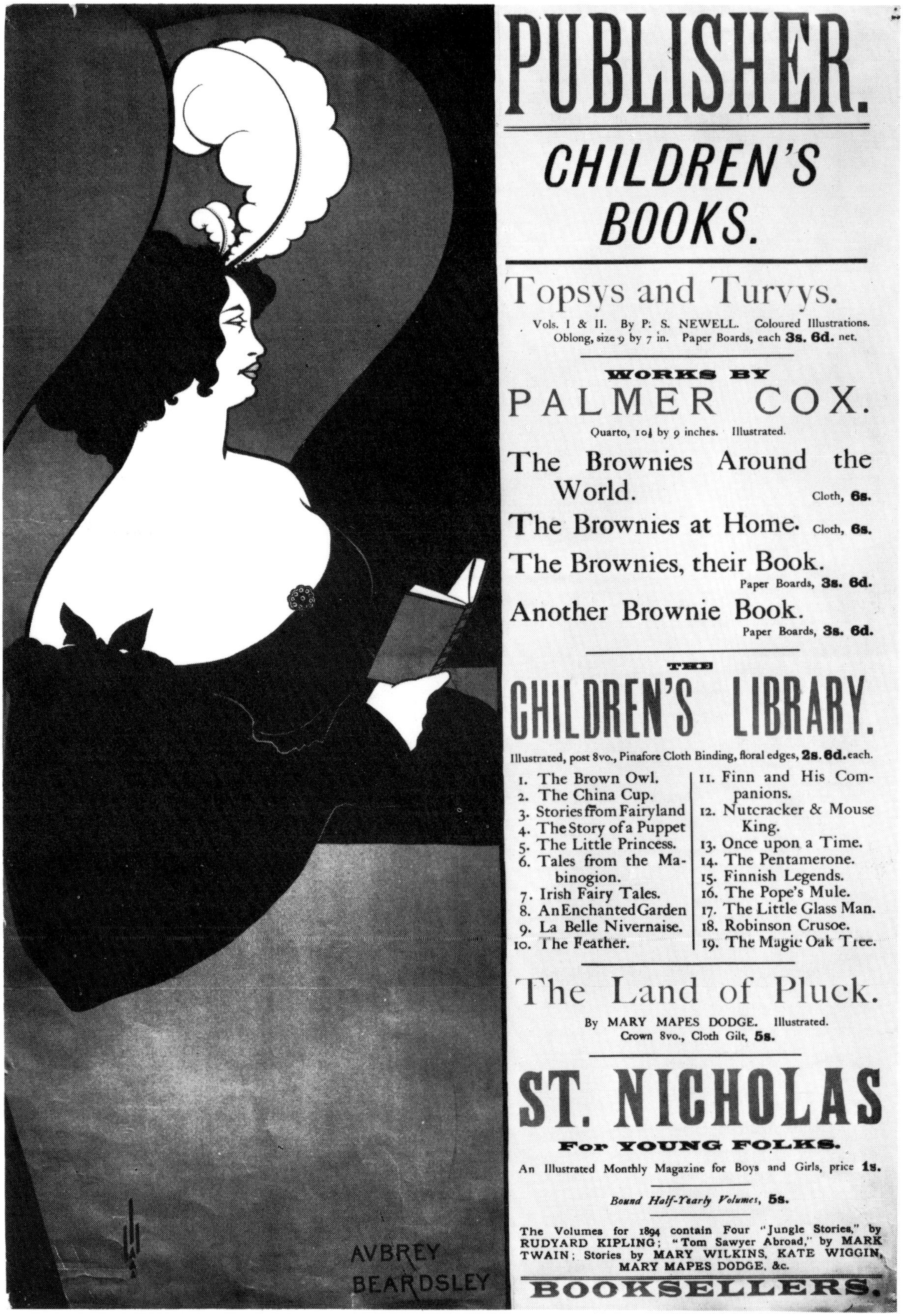

8.1 An elegant book poster design by Walter Crane for the publishers Cassell

8.2 Aubrey Beardsley's reputation as a "decadent" did not prevent recognition of his outstanding genius. This poster, advertising, rather surprisingly, children's books, perfectly illustrates the bold elegance and originality of his designs

8.3 Phineas Barnum, the American circus manager, had an intuitive flare for publicity and English advertisers learnt a good deal from him

8.4 The names of Jane Avril and Aristide Bruant, the cabaret singers, will always be associated with the superb posters designed for them by Tolouse-Lautrec

JANE
Avril
H. Stern, Paris.
1899

AMBASSADEUR
aristic
BRUAN
dans
son cabar
HLautrec

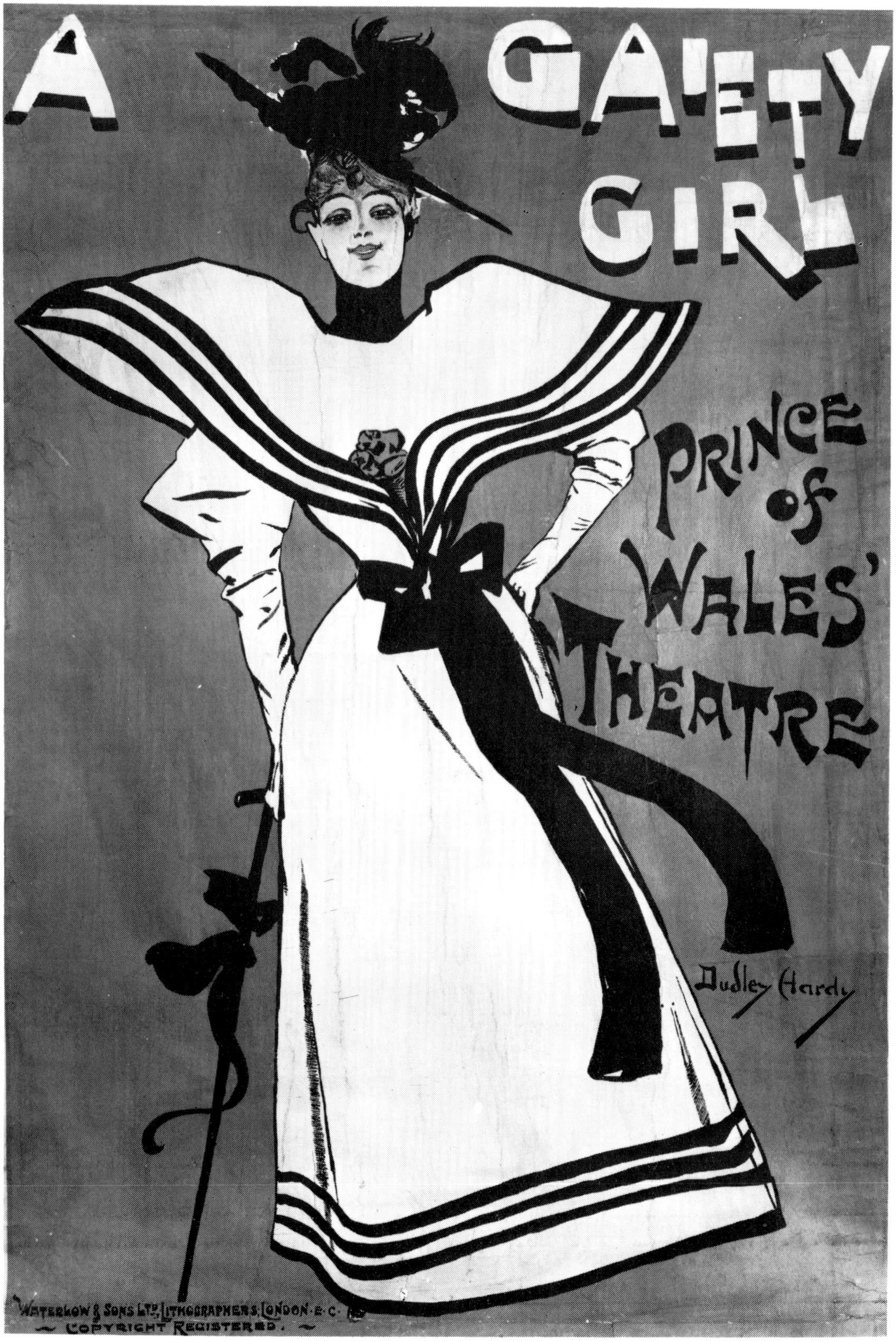

8.5 Dudley Hardy's poster "A Gaiety Girl" was one of the classic English posters of the period
8.6 The British artist Fred Walker painted one poster, commissioned to advertise a dramatised version of Wilkie Collin's novel *The Woman in White*
8.7 James Pryde and William Nicholson, working together under the soubriquet of the "Beggarstaffs", enjoyed a considerable reputation in the late 19th and early 20th centuries. This Don Quixote play-bill, one of their first great designs, shows their strong, dramatic style at its best. Such posters were a revolutionary change from the cluttered "programmes" that Victorian theatre managements usually used to advertise their productions

THE WOMAN IN WHITE
OLYMPIC THEATRE

LYCEUM
DON QUIXOTE

9 EPILOGUE

"For all sad words of tongue or pen,
The saddest are these; 'It might have been!'"

An American dream the Victorian advertisers would have understood

TABLE OF LISTED AGENCIES

It is known that there were several hundred advertising agents operating in London alone by the end of the 19th century. This check list gives the names of those discovered in the course of compiling this book with additional information where available. The abbreviation A.R. stands for Advertiser's Review. *Where not stated to the contrary the agencies were based in London.*

NAME	ADDRESS	FOUNDED	COMMENTS
Baily, A. H. & Co., General Advertising Agents	3, Royal Exchange Buildings, London	*c.* 1845	Source: *Baily's Monthly*, for 1878. "We will insert ads in the *London Gazette*, *Times* or any newspaper or publication in the kingdom. . . . we are in a position to advise as to the most suitable medium for any class of advertisements."
Bates and Hendy & Co.			Bill themselves as agents for the London Schools Board; also Rowntrees, Colman's Starch, Brown & Polsons
Benson, S. H. Advertisers' Agent	100, Fleet St from 1899: 1, Tudor St since 1909: 129, Kingsway, W.C.2	1893	Main account Bovril. Organisers of Advertisers' Exhibition, London 1899. Non-Farmer.
Bree & Co., Ltd.,	Moorgate Station Chambers, E.C.		
Brown, Gould & Co.,			
Browne, C. A. G. Advertising Agent	145, Fleet St (from Jan. 1900, 53/4 Wych St)	1895	Bill themselves as sole agent for *Canadian Home Journal*; *Canadian Manufacture.* Founded by brother of T. B. Browne
Browne, T. B. Central London Advertising Agency	163, Victoria St (Finsbury Square from 1871 to early 1880s)	1871	1886 Browne produced the famous *Bubbles* poster for his clients A. & F. Pears. CLAA also first to have a specialist trade mark department. 1888 first edition of Browne's ABC press guide, one of the largest at that time
Charles, F. C. Advertising Contractor	36–39, Maiden Lane, Strand, W.C.		Sole agent for Whitehead and Hoag Co., of New Jersey; also patentee of mirror with advertising between silver and glass
Clarke, Son & Platt		1853	
Coe, F. E. Advertising Agent	27, Bouverie St		Billed as "agent for the moderate advertiser". Published *Occasional Papers* for advertisers. Non-farmer.
Collins, Louis	Gt Marlboro' St from 1880 Wine Office Court	*c.* 1871	Published *Advertiser's Guardian*, from 1883. Passionate campaigner against corrupt practices. Sold out in 1893 to Thomas Dixon.
Crossley, Moir & Co.			Non-farmer.
Cundall, J. W.			
Dales, Reynolds & Co., 46, Cannon St	46 Cannon St E.C.		
Davis & Ornstein	28/9 St Swithin's Lane, E.C.		Non-farmers.
Dawson, H., & Co.			

NAME	ADDRESS	FOUNDED	COMMENTS
Deacon, Samuel	21, Wallbrook	as coffee house 1822; agency late 1830s	Source: Mitchell's Directory 1847. Advertising Deacon's Coffee and Boarding House of 3, Wallbrook: "Ideal temporary accommodation for gentlemen from the country, Provincial papers regularly filed. Advertisements received for every London and country newspaper at S. Deacon's, 21 Walbrook."
Dicks & Southcombe, Advertising Agents	163, The Strand		
Dixon, Thomas	197, Oxford Street	1878	Continuator of Louis Collins business and *Advertisers' Guardian*. 1901 clients Pears, Colmans, Players, Crosse & Blackwell, The Bartitusu School of Arms. Dixon's also ran a photographic studio specialising in advertisements. Non-farmer.
Duncan, J. Govane	Bolton		
Empress Bill Posting Co. Ltd.	54A, Victoria St, Blackburn, Lancs.		Registered as public company by Cartwright & Rattray, 50 Watling St, E.C.
Erwood, W. L., Ltd.	30, Fleet St, E.C.		
Gordon and Gotch	St Bride St, E.C. also of Sydney, Brisbane, Perth (Australia) & Cape Town		Source: Notice in the *Lady's Magazine* 1875
Green, Henry			
Greening & Co., Advertising Experts	20, Cecil Court, Charing Cross Rd, W.C.		
Haddon, John & Co.	Bouverie House, Salisbury Square, E.C. Now: 46/48 Grosvenor Gdns, S.W.1	1814 as printers 1880s as agency	Published *Haddon's Diary & Printers' Guide*. Listed in A.R. 1900 as one of London's largest agency's and unwilling to oppose farming.
Harrods' Advertising Agency	Knightsbridge	1899	Billed as: "Under the control of Mr Burbridge, Managing Director of Harrods."
Henderson, Advertising Contractors	2, Albemarle St, South Shields		The agency itself was advertising for: "cheap space in magazines and periodicals – state lowest terms."
Horncastles Ltd.	61, Cheapside, E.C.		Non-farmers
Irons, E. & Son, Town Criers & Bill Posters	29, Park Square, Luton		
Jones Bros., British & Foreign Advertising Contractors	39, Queen's Rd., Clifton, Bristol		Announcement in the A.R.: "We do not farm any publication. We always decline to act specially for particular papers."
Kidderminster Bill Posting Co.			
King, J. C. & Sons, Advertising Agents		1865	Source: *Advertisers' Guardian*
Lang & Co.	218, Leadenhall St E.C.		Non-farmer.

NAME	ADDRESS	FOUNDED	COMMENTS
Leng, Sir W. C. & Co.	Sheffield		
Lewis & Lowe, British Foreign and Colonial Advertisers and Newspaper Agents			Published: *The Advertiser's Guide to the Newspaper Press of the U.K.*, 1844
Lile, John H.	Ludgate Circus		Sole agent for *Sunday Companion; Home Companion; Sunday Stories*
London Press Exchange	15, The Strand		
Longman, F.			
Mather & Crowther	10–12, New Bridge St, E.C.	1850	Published *Practical Advertising*, a 400 page press directory. In A.R. for 1899 announced "Expert assistants, designers, and engravers, specially trained in advertising work."
May, C. H. & Co., General Advertising Offices	78, Grace Church St, E.C.	1846	Source: *Macmillan's Magazine* 1879. Motto: "Judicious Advertising the Keynote of Success" – same as that of U.S. Agent H. P. Hubbard.
Miers, Ernest H.	65A, Oxford St		Issued free pamphlet: *Advantageous Advertising*. Also compiled estimates and schemes without obligation.
Milton & Co.	New Inn Chambers, Wych St, WC		Non-farmers.
Mitchell, Charles Town & Country Advertising Agent	Red Lion Court	1836	Additional services: organised review copies distribution for publishers; built up specialised "mailing lists". Published *Newspaper Press Directory* 1st ed. 1846
Muller			Non-farmer.
Nelson, Advertising Contractor	25, Bouverie St		Source: *The Argosy* 1867
Pare's Advertising Agency	Augusta St, Birmingham		
Philips, F. H. B., Colonial and Indian Advertisement Agent	35D, Queen Victoria St, E.C.		Source: *Advertisers' Guardian* 1885
Potter, F. E.	56, Ludgate Hill Now: 2, Clement's Inn, W.C.2	1896	Listed by A.R. as one of London's largest and as unwilling to oppose farming. Potter founded his business in a single room in the Temple House. E.C.4.
Ratcliffe Advertising Contractor	7, George Yard, Lombard St, E.C.		Source: Note to advertisers in the *Family Guide* 1868 "All communications respecting advertisements and bills are requested to be forwarded by the 20th of the month to Mr Ratcliffe . . ."
Ratcliffe, Dunbar & Co.	3, George Yard, Lombard St, E.C.		Source: Note to advertisers in the *Englishwoman* 1895
Roberts, Henry, Bill Poster	61, Albert Rd, Middlesbrough		

NAME	ADDRESS	FOUNDED	COMMENTS
Scrivens, H. W.			Listed by A.R. as one of London's largest and unwilling to oppose farming.
Sears, F. W.			Listed by A.R. as one of London's largest and unwilling to oppose farming.
Sell, Henry	167, Fleet St	1869	Account for Mansfield Shoes of Northampton.
Simmonds & Ward, Foreign Newspaper & Advertising Agents	6, Barge Yard, Bucklesbury, London		Source: Mitchell's Directory 1846. Announcement: "Insertion of advertisements in newspapers the world over. Files of leading newspapers from every part of the world from many years back may be referred to."
Smith, James			Non-farmer.
Smith, Joseph	24, Great New St, E.C.		Source: *Advertisers' Guardian* 1885 Accounts included *Household Words*, the Magazine founded by Charles Dickens
Smith, R. Frost	64, Finsbury Pavement, E.C.		Source: Note to advertisers on LCC tramway and bus tickets Smith was agent for LCC Tramways Department at 62, Finsbury Pavement
Smith, Thomas Mutual Advertising Agency	St Brides Avenue; then: Wine Office Court then, from 1885, Fleet St	1877	Source: Advertisement in *Advertiser's Guardian* 1885. Smith published *Successful Advertising: its secrets explained.*
Stock, J. Bill Posters	3, Commercial Rd, Bedford		
Street Bros	5, Serle St	1840s	
G. Street & Co.	30, Cornhill Now: Streets House, Lawrence Lane, King St E.C.2	1860	
Tayler, Charles General Advertisement Agent		1874	Source: *Advertisers' Guardian* 1885 Tayler's make a special feature of having a telephone.
Thrower, H. S.			
Watkins & Osmond			Listed by A. R. as one of London's largest agents and unwilling to oppose farming.
R. F. White & Son	33, Fleet St Now: 72, Fleet St	after 1831	
Wilkes, C.	29, Ludgate Hill		
Willing, James Junior Ltd.			Listed by A.R. as one of London's largest agents and unwilling to oppose farming.
Wills, M. W.			Won Schweppes account 1899
Wilson, A. J. & Co. Ltd.	168, Clerkenwell Rd		Non-farmers.
Wilson, Hartnell & Co.	Dublin		
Wilson, F.			Non-farmers

LIST OF PUBLICATIONS

Most of the material for this study of advertising in the reign of Victoria has been derived from a host of short items in the magazines and newspapers of the period. There are very few recent books on the subject; by far the best treatment is in the relevant chapters of E. S. Turner's excellent work *The Shocking History of Advertising* (London 1952; Penguin Books, 1968). The most comprehensive treatment of the development of poster art in France is Jane Abdy's *The French Poster* (London 1969); the pioneer work in this field is *Les Affiches Illustres* (Paris 1886) by Ernest Maindron.

The following list comprises the magazines, directories and journals that contain articles or chapters explicitly concerned with the techniques of advertising or its history.

The Advertiser's Guide to Publicity, Anonymous (Birmingham 1887)
The Advertiser's Guardian, Louis Collins (London 1883)
The Advertiser's Guide to the Newspaper Press of the United Kingdom, Lewis and Lowe (London 1844)
The Newspaper Press Directory, Charles Mitchell (London 1846)
The Philosophy of Advertising, Henry Sell (London 1882)
Succesful Advertising : Its Secrets Explained, Thomas Smith (London 1878)
The Advertiser's Review (London 1899–)
The Poster (London 1898–)
The Poster Collector's Circular (London 1899)

INDEX

Italicised figures refer to colour or black and white illustrations